WOODWORKING PROJECTS FOR BEGINNERS

More than 100 Easy Projects that Teach the Basics with Detailed Plans, Secrets, Techniques, Diagrams and Illustrations.

Recommended Tools and Accessories to Use

By

Stanton tools Wood

© **Copyright 2020**

All rights reserved.

This document is intended to provide accurate and reliable information on the subject and problem. The publication is sold with the notion that the publisher is not required to provide officially authorized or otherwise qualified accounting services. When legal or professional advice is necessary, a person practicing within a profession should be ordered from the Declaration of Principles accepted and approved equally by the American Bar Association Committee and the Committee of Publishers and Associations.

It is not legal for any part of this document to be reproduced, duplicated or transmitted either by electronic means or in printed format. This publication is strictly forbidden to be recorded, and any storage of this document is not permitted unless the publisher has written permission. All rights reserved—all rights.

The details given herein shall be accurate and consistent in that the recipient's readers are only and totally responsible for any fault, in terms of un-attention or otherwise, for any use or misuse of all policies, procedures or directions found within it. Under no circumstances shall the publisher be held responsible for any reparations, damages or monetary losses arising out of the material, directly or indirectly.

All copyrights not held by the publisher belong to the respective authors.

The material in this section is only accessible for knowledge purposes and is standardized as such. The information is delivered without a contract or any kind of guarantee.

The trademarks used shall be without any consent, and the trademark publication shall be without permission or endorsement by the trademark owner. All trademarks and brands in this book are owned and not affiliated with this document and are only for clarification purposes.

TABLE OF CONTENTS

INTRODUCTION 8

Basics of woodworking 9

   1. Know Your Wood 10

   2. Set up a Dedicated Workspace 13

   3. Respect the Tools and Practice Woodworking Safety 14

   5. Start With a Project & Learn to Read Woodworking Plans 16

   6. Understand the Woodworking Process 17

   7. Master the Cut: How to Measure and Cut Wood Accurately 18

   8. Learn How to Assemble and Join Wood...............19

   9. Protect Your Creations: Best Practices for Sanding & Finishing Wood 20

Different Types of Wood & Their Uses 21

   The Three Main Types of Wood 21

   Softwoods 22

   Hardwoods..23

   Engineered Wood: Manufactured Wood Products..24

   Types of Wood for Woodworking, Furniture & Building 25

Must-Have Tools For Woodworking 64

   SAWS USED FOR WOODWORKING 66

FILING, PLANING, AND SANDING SUPPLIES USED IN WOODWORKING 75

ASSEMBLY TOOLS FOR WOODWORKING 79

TOOLS FOR MEASUREMENT AND ANGLES 84

OTHER NECESSITIES FOR SUCCESSFUL WOODWORKING PROJECTS 86

Repair and Maintenance of Woodwork Tools 88

Guide to Buying Lumber for woodworking 91

WHY IS THE ACTUAL SIZE OF THE BOARD DIFFERENT THAN THE STATED SIZE? 92

WHAT KIND OF WOOD SHOULD YOU BUY FOR YOUR PROJECT? 94

HOW DO YOU CHOOSE STRAIGHT BOARDS? 100

HOW TO STORE BOARDS TO MINIMIZE WARPING 101

Woodworking Measuring and marking-out guide 102

Marking-out tools 104

Measuring and marking wood before cutting. 106

Essential woodworking cuts you should know. 107

Woodworking Tricks and tips for beginners 110

Wood Layout - Triangle Registration 110

Marking Cut Lines 111

Straight Lines on Dowels 112

Story Stick 113

Drill Depth 113

Glue Cleanup 114

- Keep Slippery Glue-Ups Steady 114
- Wax Paper Cover 115
- Hold Glue-Ups Instantly 115
- Sandpaper Organization 117

Wood Glues 118
- Choosing the Right Type of Wood Glue 119
- How Long Does Wood Glue Last? 124

Sanding and Preparing Wood Before Staining 126
- Sandpaper or Power Tools 126
- Sand with the Grain 127
- Removing the Dust 128

List Of Woodworking Projects for Beginners 130
- WOODEN CUTTING BOARD 130
- DIY PET BED 133
- DIY WOOD DOORMAT 139
- Wooden Beer Caddy 141
- Vintage Step Stool 148
- WOODEN SOFA SLEEVE WITH CUP HOLDER 152
- More projects to try out 161

Common Woodworking Pitfalls and How to Avoid Them
.... 163
- Uneven or blotchy finish 164
- Drawers or doors that don't fit 164
- A table that rocks 165

Stain that doesn't take 167

Sanding that makes the wood fuzzy 167

Joints that don't fit together 168

Tabletops that aren't flat 169

Wood that splits when being cut 170

Joints that are too loose 171

CONCLUSION 172

INTRODUCTION

Have you ever thought about the scope a person could mean by simply saying, "I'm a woodworker?"

Back in the day, when almost everything was made from wood, we had many different names for those who worked wood like collaborator, wheelwright, luthier, woodcarver, pattern maker, carpenter, and many more. We now have a boat builder in our eZine — a trade once the sole domain of woodworkers. It is very remarkable that woodworkers make items as diverse as wooden spoons and boats which can sail all over the world.

It is also a bold step to decide to become a woodworker. It's friendly, enjoyable, and even quite profitable! But for beginners, woodwork is also the other way round, since a certain degree of experience is required before the first successful projects are started. This book will clarify the foundations of what you need to make sure you start the right way and really enjoy the process.

BASICS OF WOODWORKING

There are some important things to learn as a beginner in woodworking and I hope this woodworking guide will help you prevent facing all possible pitfalls.

Don't worry: Everyone starts somewhere to be a woodworker. The first time a hammer is picked up, most people don't become master carpenters. It can be annoying to feel frustrated at first, but you can soon create things you never thought possible with just a little practice.

Many new beginners fail because they never took the time to learn the fundamentals of what they need to know when they are creating with wood. They always like to compete with someone who is really experienced and wonder why they're behind so much. However, in most of these cases, you often see someone with more than 30 years of experience and practice!

The more time you study fundamentals and practice skills, the greater outcomes you can get, as most hobbies or even careers. All skills will be easily built if you have patience and commitment.

When you put your woodwork skills into practice, you WILL see results! Learning these simple principles now will help you to early learn good habits to successfully and frustration-free projects.

These basics will help you to find everything you need from the start to the end of your first woodworking project – along with many helpful tips to ensure that you remain organized, safe and save time on the road.

1. KNOW YOUR WOOD

Comprehension of wood and building forms

There are many people that immerse themselves in a new woodworking project as a beginner without really knowing various types of wood and whether the wood is also the best material for their project.

Before you start woodwork, the first thing to learn is to consider the different forms of wood and the properties of wood.

It is also very important to learn why wood is doing things. If you wonder why your boards split or why the wood splits every time you drill, you may not have taken sufficient time to understand how wood is behaving fully!

Studying wood gives you a huge advantage in your woodworking and also helps you prevent constant errors.

Some types of wood are better suited than others for certain ventures. Some types of wood can be lightweight and simple to use, but some can be very heavy. Strong woods such as oak will make you face their own unique challenges.

One thing to remember is that wood comes from nature and nature presents several different types of trees! A few of the many types of bodies of wood are pine, maple, oak, cherry, poplar and birch. Some of these forests are more suitable than others for various ventures.

For instance, if you know that wood is growing and shrinking according to climate temperature and humidity, this will help you prepare your wood by making sure your wood is indoors prior to cutting and building.

If you understand a bit about wood grain, it can help you to know a bit more about how to split and crack the wood.

Do you also know that wood is absorbent when you are exploring the various adhesives and wood glues to combine wood? This consistency is also useful when you want to paint or stain wood.

In addition to only wood forms and wood resources, it is beneficial to understand important issues about the purchasing of wood and wood products in a woodworking shop.

From your standard dimensional wood to the finished wood goods. There are other things to remember, such as lumber manufactured under strain, plywood, organized strand board (OSB) and fibre-board of medium density (MDF).

It could at first seem daunting, but it can be very helpful to know all your wood forms! Please spend some time in a local wood store and explore the different wood types available. Take the time to figure out how wood works when you deal with it.

2. SET UP A DEDICATED WORKSPACE

One important thing to remember before you begin designing projects is how you plan to arrange and set up your workroom.

You don't have to dedicate a whole garage or shed to woodworking and construction projects – but you want to have a way to store your tools and building material carefully. Many woodworking projects do need space – particularly if you intend to create big bulky stuff such as furniture.

Organizing and building a room will save you a lot of stress and time.

I can't say how many carpenters I know struggle for no good reason just because they're disorganized! Perhaps you know someone like that-they can't remember where they put the device they need to use, or they must clean up a huge amount of material from an entirely unrelated project just to get to their workstation.

This dilemma can be avoided now, and healthy organizational habits can start early. Do not wait until the "actual shop room" is available. Organize now, and you can create something easily anywhere. You don't need much space – but there needs to be a special place to arrange it easily so you can find it and use it safely.

3. Respect the Tools and Practice Woodworking Safety

Until we get to something, you must learn to respect the tools and ALWAYS practice woodwork with protection.

Safety can sound repetitive or even unnecessary, but many "know better" type of people still end up every year in the emergency room for not using equipment correctly and for neglecting basic safety requirements.

Most injuries can be prevented, and the practice of safety takes no extra time, but it is simply a question of establishing good habits and practices NOW when you are a beginner.

Learn the Different Types of Tools and Their Uses

There are thousands of tools for your projects to choose from, and of course, some tools are better than others for some projects. Although you can know basics like "screwdriver" or "saw," these items may vary greatly, as there are different styles!

Another thing to remember is whether you want to use power tools vs hand tools. Many woodworkers use both, and just understanding all of the different choices out there will allow you to decide which ones would be most beneficial.

There is a wide range of woodworking projects, and many great tools are available to create all of them. The crucial question to ask before buying any tool first: What kind of stuff do you want to build?

An understanding of what you want to create will help you decide which resources are right for your work. It allows you to manage your production and inventory budget effectively.

In addition to simple tools, which are a must for any timber worker, you can need a lot of specialized tools at some level.

- Cabinet Making Tools
- Furniture Making Tools
- Wood Carving Tools

It saves you a lot of time and money, later on, to know about the various types of devices. You can remember that you don't need 12 separate types of saws – all you need for now is a single table saw or circular screw.

That brings us to the next thing woodworkers must learn.

5. Start With a Project & Learn to Read Woodworking Plans

It's a lot easier to learn with a project that was first developed and validated. Often these woodworking plans also include a setlist of materials and procedural guidance for a step by step construction of the piece.

Woodworking plans can be difficult to read and understand. Most plans of woodworking at least include a list of materials and the size of every piece to be made. This alone will save you a lot of stress and time!

6. UNDERSTAND THE WOODWORKING PROCESS

You have the room, have the equipment, know the safety tips, have a project – now it's time to really dig into the process and learn how to build it from start to finish.

In most woodworking designs, all steps are essentially the same from start to finish. Sometimes, every time you make something different, you follow the same steps. Understanding the woodworking process will save you a lot of time and frustration while attempting to build your own creations.

Although each woodworker has its own routine and way of doing things, they typically follow these steps in the construction of a project:

- Choose a Project
- Gather Supplies & Materials

- Make a Cut List
- Review the Build Strategy
- Measure & Cut the Wood
- Assemble the Wood
- Apply a Protective Finish to the Wood

After the basic steps and the routine, you should excel in a successful system for whole projects. If you try to do all these things simultaneously, you will be more likely to make mistakes or become disorganized.

7. Master the Cut: How to Measure and Cut Wood Accurately

Another important thing is to know how to calculate correctly when you are new to woodworking. If you do not know the tricks to make even and clean cuts every time, it can be very difficult to try to get two different boards of the same size.

Learning how to cut wood as a beginner precisely would not only save you time but also save you a lot of money. Often you will save a lot if you buy longer boards you can cut yourself.

8. Learn How to Assemble and Join Wood

While wood and tools are important, the basics of how to combine two pieces of wood properly are also very important! Knowing the tips and tricks to put all the wood bits together makes your life much easier.

It all depends on the project you are working on, but you have to learn several different types of fasteners and adhesives. There are also some ways to incorporate wood to different finishes.

There are also several different assembly approaches that all put together make the process even more enjoyable. For starters, before you try to put something together, you probably want to learn how to master dry fitting. Yet woodworking clamps are your best friend in almost all situations.

9. Protect Your Creations: Best Practices for Sanding & Finishing Wood

If your project is completed successfully, you are ready to proceed to the next step, which is to sand the part and provide security for your project.

As a woodworker, understanding the fundamentals of sanding and completing your woodworking projects is very important. It means that the designs succeed and will be appreciated for several more years.

Sanding furniture provides a good smooth finish if you choose to use a clear cover, stain or paint the piece - it will make sure that no one gets splinter while attempting to use the product you have made. There are a variety of ways of sanding wood, whether you are using sandpaper or investing in anything like this.

When the piece has been sanded, the next move is a protective finish. The type of protective finish you use also depends on the way the item will be used and on the type of projects you have made.

Different Types of Wood & Their Uses

Learning the many different wood types and their uses will help you select the right wood for your next project. If you create something out of wood or just choose wood furniture for your home, this list of several types of wood will ensure that you can select wood that will please you,

Wood is available in various shapes and sizes. Since wood comes from trees and there are several varieties of trees, it is not surprising that we have a great range of woods for building.

The Three Main Types of Wood

It is important to understand the three fundamental types of wood you will find, before we get to all the various wood varieties and their common uses. There are three types: softwoods, hardwoods and timber. Each of these wood types can be used in many ways.

SOFTWOODS

The wood that is milled from coniferous trees is also known as softwood. Coniferous trees are historically classified as gymnosperms, all the trees that have needles that produce cones. Pin, Cedar, Fir, Spruce and Redwood are examples of common softwood trees used in woodworking, building and furniture.

Are Softwoods Softer Than Hardwoods?

Unlike common opinion, softwoods are not called 'softwood' because they are 'soft.' Although it is true that certain hardwood types are hard and thus harder to work with, there is nothing in relation to the distinction between hardwood and softwood or that it is harder to work with. Most hardwoods are softer than softwoods.

How Are Softwoods Like Pine, Cedar, Spruce, Fir and Redwood Used?

Most softwoods in many different building applications are solid and widely used. Spruce, Pine and Fir (SPF) are also sold in home improvement centres as SPF dimensional wood. These trees are also used in designing new buildings and building structures.

Many of these forests, and particularly cypress softwoods, are known for being resistant to rot and insects. This makes trees like cedar and redwood perfect for outdoor projects like decks and furniture.

HARDWOODS

Hardwoods come from some trees that don't grow needles or cones. Such plants are commonly called leafy plants, more scientifically known as angiosperms. Hardwoods are leaves and seed-producing trees.

Oak, maple, cherry, mahogany and walnut are common species of hardwood. The hardwood species are not inherently stronger than the softwoods ones, but many species are known for their unique and distinct patterns of the wood grain.

Many forests are often called hardwoods, not leafy trees, such as bamboo and palm trees. These plants are scientifically known as monocotyledons, but have some of the same hardwood characteristics and are also categorized as monocotyledons. The next type of engineered wood can often be Bamboo and Palm.

ENGINEERED WOOD: MANUFACTURED WOOD PRODUCTS

The third type of wood that you will find is processed wood. Engineered wood is not naturally developed in the forest.

Such boards are typically made of wood that is handled to create certain characteristic. Such products are also known as composite wood and are mostly made of sawmill waste wood.

Processed wood is also treated by chemical treatment or by heat to create a wood product that can meet certain measurements that are difficult to obtain by definition.

Popular examples are Plywood, Oriented Strand Board, Medium Density Fiber Board and Composite Board. Wood veneers may also often be categorized as wood made because they often have to be manipulated by using professional techniques of cutting or joining parts in order to achieve a certain size or grain style.

Now that we know these three key wood types, we are ready to begin discussing all the various wood types you may find and what they are used for.

TYPES OF WOOD FOR WOODWORKING, FURNITURE & BUILDING

While there are three major wood types, there are thousands of wood varieties and wood species. In this section, we cover the most common woods you can find in construction and woodworking. For each wood variety, we provide an overview of its common characteristics and for which each wood type is best suited.

All forests are listed in alphabetical order. If you are looking for a particular wood type, you can find it easily on this list.

Alder Wood

Alder is a hardwood that slowly increases in popularity due to its natural elegance, durability and versatility. It is more popular in California's northwest and Canada 's southwest areas. This belongs to the same family as the birch tree and also has similar applications.

When freshly cut, Alder appears nearly white, but quickly becomes moist, brown sweet once exposed to air and sunlight. This medium-density wood generally has a straight grain and is easy to cut, turn and process.

This wood also works well with a number of finishing procedures. Alder wood has a very smooth surface that can be painted or coated quickly when sanded.

The Alder tree does not grow in diameter or height very much, so it is important to consider it if you need very large solid parts as they can be harder and so more expensive to obtain.

Alder is also used in furniture and cabinet making. It is also famous for picture frames and other objects.

Perhaps one of Alder Wood's most advanced applications is the hard electric guitar shell. Alder wood offers a clean sound which is difficult to recreate with other woods. Alder is also more attractive for its sound than exotic hardwoods such as mahogany in electric guitars.

Ash

Ashwood can be very difficult to locate at present, in particular, due to the recent problems with the Emerald Ash borer, an invasive species that caused the premature death of many of these trees. If you live in regions where the Ash trees are native and grow abundantly, finding this wood will be easier than living in areas that are not.

Ash imitates the same strength and characteristics of white oak but usually comes at a lower price if you can find it near you at the local wooden yard. This wood can be easily painted and used for different types of projects.

Aspen

Aspen is a light-colored wood that paints and stains well. Sometimes this wood looks or sounds like a soft texture.

Aspen is a hardwood grown in Northeastern America but can be hard to find. This is usually used for very specific projects where Aspen wood is the only one suitable because of its relatively restricted availability.

The building of saunas is one of the most advanced uses of Aspen wood. This wood doesn't heat up, and with minimal swelling or motion, it can withstand the moisture well. Since it does not conduct heat quickly, it is also often used for matches production.

Such characteristics also make Aspen attractive to use in furniture to create drawer slides as this can minimize sticking. This wood is also fragrant and taste-free, making it suitable for cookware and kitchenware.

Balsa Wood

Balsa is a very soft hardwood usually used for hobbies and crafts. Most fine woodworkers tend to have a negative look at balsa wood as it is not very solid. It is often underestimated and has many practical applications.

Many of us use balsa wood for the first time in childhood building projects and sets. Balsa wood may be considered children's play by the most skilled woodworkers, but perhaps the catalyst for woodwork and construction.

This wood also has a very rich history, especially as it was often used in aircraft and ships as a replacement during World War I and World War II.

Balsa wood is typically transported from South America and Central America into North America. It grows very fast but has a relatively short lifespan, and most trees only yield usable wood before they are ten years old.

This type of wood is extremely busy, and many people are surprised to learn that it is often used in building rafts, life storage facilities and other kinds of floating objects. Surfboards are a fine example of beautifully crafted Balsa wood projects.

Balsa wood is a small, usually not very strong wood. This is why many people prefer basswood and birch over balsa wood for any type of project that can handle weight or stress.

On the other hand, if you need to make something from wood that can crack or break quickly, such as a theatre and film set, balsa is a great choice.

The wood grain can be conveniently painted or dyed to be used as a veneer to achieve a number of cheap looks.

When balsa wood is used in building projects, glue is often needed because the wood does not play too well with clasps or twines. Quite small bits of balsa wood can sometimes only be cut with a decent saw or craft knife.

Bamboo

While Bamboo is technically a grass and not a wood, due to the strength and density of the plant stems, it can be used for many items. Bamboo grows abundantly in tropical climates, and several different species that vary widely between regions are available.

The plant in Bamboo has a large, hollow stem. Such stems may be used as-is or cut into very thin, narrow strips to create a furnace. The furnace product from the stems is made of wood, such as splice wood.

While people may think that Bamboo is light, soft and easy to bend or cut, that isn't the case. Bamboo is better than hardwood red oak or maple because it is equally hard and solid. The high-density grass can be rough on equipment sometimes.

Bamboo stalks are popular with garden furniture, fences and privacy screens. You can also see bamboo in wardrobes, fine furnishings and even hardwood floors.

The natural waxy surface of Bamboo is part of what makes it able to withstand decay outdoors. Whether you choose to dye, paint or glue bamboo, you have first to sand the wood to ensure that it is painted or glued in. If used outdoors, most bamboos should be sealed and protected for longevity.

Humidity can cause the bamboo to swell or shrink, so it is best to acclimatize before cutting, particularly if you are in a colder and drier environment than the native of the plant.

Basswood

Basswood is a very light creamy wood with very compact and straight grains. This wood is not susceptible to distortion or movement when it is properly acclimated and dried.

Basswood is a favoured hardwood for woodcutters. It is also a common option for people who like miniature woodworking and construction models. Woodturners also prefer to work with basswood because it is easy to use.

There is no odour, taste or allergens in the wood, so it is a common option for food storage boxes or even for use in kitchen utensils. Basswood is easy to find and it's usually cheap.

It can be difficult to stain uniformly. The natural finish with a safe, clear oil coat is typically better appreciated, or wood is finished. Many decorative painters enjoy working with basswood projects because it allows a very smooth finish after it has been prepared.

Beechwood

Beech is a hardwood which is mostly used in wood veneers, furnishings, and woodworking items. This cream-tone wood has a clear grain pattern, generally straight and close, and is rarely spotted in brown. This wood is very soft but typically has a yellow-reddish colour.

This is a sturdy wood known for its ability to bend quickly. That's why beech is a perfect choice to make all sorts of interior furnishings, including chairs and other curved pieces. Such benefit can also contribute to honey wood being often exposed to movement, shrinkage and swelling in the weather, or unexpected moisture.

Beech is also used in pianos, which are used for the piano mechanism's bridge and pin parts.

Beechwood is in the cheapest category of hardwoods, it can be found in a wide variety of sizes and can be used as a furnace. This wood can be used fairly easily as long as the tools are sharp. If needed, it can be glued and painted without too much troube.

Birch Wood

Birch is a hardwood easy to find and also one of the most accessible types of hardwood in local woodlands and in households.

Birch is very powerful, and almost anything you can imagine can be used for. Many people use birch as an alternative to Oak, that is cheaper.

One thing about birch wood, though, is that it can be very hard to paint. Often stalking can lead to blotchy patches that look uneven. Birch is an ideal and cost-effective hardwood for your project to paint.

California Redwood

The redwood trees of California are known for their large size and red colour. This has a fascinating grain pattern and likes its Cedar counterparts, and because of the weather-resistance, Redwood is very suitable for outdoor applications.

Redwood is often used for railway links and ties, it is also popular for building storage walls, decks, and garden lines. Redwood is also an excellent choice for chairs, tables, and large cabinet designs.

Cedar Wood

Many people know cedar not only because of its interesting grain and colour but also because of its aromatic smell, which repelled pests and moths. The aromatic scent and bug repelling properties are the reason why in closets and storage chests, it is sometimes a popular option.

Cedar is also the perfect choice for outdoor construction projects. This wood is often seen as red resistant and can be quite resistant to the harsh weather outside. For this reason, many people use outdoor cedar, such as decks, furnishings, fencing and decorative façades.

There are several cedar wood species, which belong to the Cypress family. For specific applications, some cedar species are better than others.

Common Cedarwood Varieties:

- Western Red Cedar
- Eastern Red Cedar
- Northern White Cedar
- Yellow Cedar

- Spanish Cedar

Although many people love cedar for its aromatic characteristics, it is important to note that some people can be allergic to natural oils. If you plan to use cedarwood, you must wear gloves and wear a mask to reduce sawdust inhalation.

Cedar should not be used for kitchen utensils or any other project which may be used with food or have prolonged contact with the skin because of the high risk of irritation.

Cherry

Cherry is a stunning wood that comes from the fruit tree of the American Black Cherry. This wood also starts as a light rose colour that becomes dark and over time, reddish. Cherry wood may often be seen in black, which is usually caused by overtime mineral deposits.

You may want to take some time to pick cherry wood and try to make sure that all the pieces that you choose fit. Cherry can be polished, but most people prefer their natural state and give it a simple protective finish to differentiate the beauty of wood and natural pathways with ageing.

Douglas Fir

Fir is another great economic and efficient softwood for starting woodworking projects. Fir is typically a good choice for painting projects as it can often be hard to stain and does not have much wood grain.

Some varieties of fir have a very dense wood grain, which gives them a little more strength and stability than pine. Fir is widely used for building and utilities, where the finishing of the natural wood grain is not especially necessary.

Ebony

Ebony wood is easy to identify because it is one of a few woods that really are black. This is a very thick hardwood with many features that make it attractive in several wood carving and woodwork projects.

Ebony is a protected species and is also heavily monitored worldwide. Cameroon is the only country in which wood can be harvested legally, and harvesting is not always desirable.

It can sometimes be very hard to obtain ebony wood for this reason. The tree is growing very slowly, contributing to its scarcity. Ebony has traditionally been used in the manufacturing of musical instruments used to produce black keys on pianos and guitar fretboards.

Older pianos and no longer playable musical instruments can be a fascinating source of recycling of old ebony wood. Antique pianos would most possibly have very solid ebony keys, although sometimes with other wood types black keys had been made.

As a sculpture medium, ebony produces a beautiful finish and can hold details. Some woodworkers recommend only hand tools with ebony, as the stiffness and strength of the instrument can be difficult.

Ebony should not be sprayed so that it can be a task to glue occasionally. It is most likely finished with very fine sanding, buffing and waxing. Any type of sealant or varnish with this wood should be avoided.

Most cabinet makers who wish to manufacture the same look as ebony, but instead prefer cherry or walnut to use more sustainable woods and then paint it with dark black colour. This not only saves costs and encourages sustainability but can also be much less difficult than ebony to create with cherry and walnut.

Hardboard (HDF: High-Density Fiber Board widely known)

Hardboard is a wood component made of tightly compressed wood fibres. It can be made by using a dry or wet process, and the process used decides whether the wood has two "good sides" or only one "good side."

Hardboard has a distinctive fabric and has no grain pattern, but it is usually matched with a dark wood veneer. It is possible to paint a hardboard, although surface preparations usually need to be carried out so that the paint does not peel or chip later.

Often chalkboards are made from a kind of wood, such as hardboard, and then coated in flat paint. This can be a very quick and easy way to make your board, and you can always create a decorative framework with a nicer wood.

Hardboard comes in many forms and has various names. Masonite is a form of hardboard widely used in theatre's building sets and props. This is frequently used also by building and moving companies to cover floor surfaces temporarily and to allow movement of products on dollies or chariots.

Tempered hardboard means the board has been treated and baked with linens oil. This process can help to improve its durability, moisture resistance and strength.

Pegboard, also known as Perforated Hard Board, is a tempered hardboard which has uniformly boiled trousers. These holes are normally 1/8 of an inch in diameter and generally have a distance of 1/4" between the holes. Pegboard is commonly used as display racks for storage, and it can be a perfect way to organize your garage or workbench.

Although hardboard is not the first option to build luxury furniture, it can help to create certain pieces of furniture economically, including TV stands and entertainment centres. It is also used as a backrest for clothes and cabinets, particularly as these components are typically against a wall and are not visible.

Hardboard is available in almost every home improvement store, and you can also order it online with trust. Since the wood component is produced equally, you can easily order online without worrying about flaws or differences between pieces, such as natural wood.

Fibre Cement Board: Hardy Board

It is necessary not to confuse hardboard or Hardie backer board. The names can sound equally confusing, but they are very, very different.

Hardie board is a composite building material, the fibre cement board company. The reason fibre cement board is widely referred to as the Hardie board is that the James Hardie Company is one of the largest manufacturers of this commodity.

Cement fibre board is primarily made of cement and cellulose fibres. While it is an engineered surface, it is usually not known as wood and is not used as a wood substitute in most applications.

The most common use of fibre cement boards is as a substratum for flooring and walls. The James Hardie company also produces cement decking and siding carbon material.

Larch / Tamarack

The Larch wood, also known as Tamarack wood, belongs to the Larix tree genus. Larix laricina is the most known Tamarack variety in North America. Across Eurasia, Larix decidua is more common and more frequently known as Larch.

Larch trees are a rare type of tree in the Cypress family, technically a softwood. It meets both the criteria to be classified as both softwoods and hardwoods, which makes that specific tree unusual as a softwood.

It is a coniferous tree which has needles and produces cones, but the tree species is categorized as leaves, as it releases its similar needles as many trees lose their leaves in autumn. It is also known as leaves.

It is one of the strongest and toughest among softwoods. It has many common characteristics of its Redwood and Cedar cousins since it is in the Cypress family of trees.

Tamarack typically has a reddish-brown colour and is rotting and pest resistant, making it the ideal alternative for projects outdoors. The straight grain and hardness of the wood will make it easier to break and chipped.

It is important to note that as is common for trees in the Cypress family, this wood can cause irritation or allergic sensitivity. The resins and oils of plants that make it attractive for its rotten resistance often cause problems for some people.

This wood should therefore usually be reserved for applications that do not come into sustained contact with the skin. As you work with these trees, you will need to ensure that your current interaction with wood's resins and oils is limited by fatigue from inhaling sawdust and wearing gloves.

Luan (also spelt Lauan)

Luan can usually be found as a plateau made of Shorea wood native to the Philippines and other countries of south-east Asia. The Lauan tree is a flowering plant in the Shorea family. Although it is technically a hardwood, we will most likely find wood in non-natural forms like plywood.

Usually, this plate is only available in very small parts, usually 1/8th inch, or 1/4th inch thick. It is typically available in large 4' x 8' sheets even if some shops sell smaller pre-cut products.

This wood is very flexible and easy to bend. This gives it a special property to make miniatures and models very useful. It is also common for use in other craft or hobby projects as lightweight and relatively inexpensive with reliable availability.

It is important to note that because Luan is willing to bend and comes in a very thin piece, it must not be used in applications where the pressure is high, or the structural strength is necessary.

Luan is usually called Philippine Mahogany, but it is important to know that it has a direct connection to direct Mahogany Wood, which we are going to discuss next.

Mahogany

Mahogany is a beautiful, exotic hardwood and luxury furniture wood. The wood also starts with a pink tone that over time deepens and darkens.

It is easy to work with and beautifully stain – sometimes only a basic coat of oil is required here. Mahogany is lighter than many of the hardwoods, making it easier on your players.

Many manufacturers of musical instruments still use Mahogany to make guitars and pianos because it acoustically creates a clear sound.

Mahogany wood is usually imported from South and Central America, so it can be expensive to buy and hard to find. Such plants are known as Mahogany Tropical.

You may want to make sure that the wood you choose is harvested sustainably if you want to use it for a project. Sadly, the demand for this wood can also lead to major deforestation if it is not harvested from sustainable sources.

Other styles of mahogany are also available. Australian Mahogany has similar characteristics but is somewhat different because it comes from the Eucalyptus plant family. Philippine mahogany is very different too and is generally seen as a very "cheap" type of wood such as Luan.

Maple

Maple is a beautiful hardwood mostly used in applications that demonstrate the natural grain of the wood. Maple is primarily grown in tropical forests in North America.

There are several different types of maple trees, which is why you can find two simple varieties to choose from when you shop for Maple: soft or hard. Strong maple is from the Sugar Maple Variety, which usually is made of red maple trees.

Red Maple, also called soft maple, is typically the best choice for woodworking since tools are much easier to use.

Sugar maple can be difficult to cut and work with, and it is also known as hard maple. Because of its hardness, Sugar Maple is a common option for hardwood floors. This type of maple can be misused to hold furniture on and without indenting or scuffing.

MDF: Medium Density Fiberboard

Medium-density fiberboard generally referred to as MDF, is another wood product like HDF or a high-density fiberboard but has a lower overall density.

The fibre density variations make MDF more suitable than hardboard for various applications. MDF has more acoustic and isolating properties, for example, and often it is used in applications where desired, such as inside a speaker.

MDF is generally not a desirable woodworking product. It can be difficult to work with, and many people are worried about chemicals, especially formaldehyde, that are leached into the atmosphere.

MDF is one of those things you should study if you are thinking of using it, but most of the time, you just would not want it to be used if you could stop it.

Oak

Perhaps one of the most revered hardwoods, oak is a very common choice for woodworkers, especially in construction furniture and heirlooms of high quality, which can last for generations.

The two wide varieties of oak wood are white oak and red oak. Red oak has a reddish colour hint and is generally the most available in most wooden shops. Red oak is significantly thicker than white oak, which makes the processing simpler.

White oak is a really strong wood and it's a perfect alternative for hardwood floors. Elm is also resistant to rot and decay, and it can be used in external applications for proper care and sealing.

It is important to know that you need to be acclimatized to your shop before working with oak. Oak is susceptible to swelling and shrinkage depending on temperature and humidity levels, therefore, particularly when using it for flooring or making containers such as wooden bodies to hold water, it is important to take account of this.

Oak is easy to stain and is, therefore, a perfect alternative for different stained finishes. You can also paint oak, but most woodworkers agree it is a waste, particularly if you can use similarly strong woods that are cheaper, if you intend to paint over a beautiful natural wood grain and cover it.

Oriented Strand Board (OSB)

The oriented beach board, more commonly referred to as OSB, is a type of wood product which is often used as an alternative to splicing wood. This wood is made from wood strands arranged in a cross-hatched arrangement in which the resin is mixed, and a thermal heating process is undertaken.

The boards are usually uniform in size and thickness, although their texture is very distinct. OSB can often be painted, but it is difficult to avoid the texture of wood strands.

OSB is frequently found to be considerably cheaper than plain wood. For this reason, OSB is found in new residential buildings. Most people use it as boards, walls, and roofs sheathing.

OSB is also used to make low-cost laminate furniture. For most instances, the OSB is protected by a veneer. Only where the end grain is visible can it be understood that it is OSB, as seen in the photo example.

Although these pieces of furniture are not expensive, they are certainly of less quality than those made from natural woods. A simple hammer tap may cause a poorly designed laminate piece of furniture made of OSB to collapse completely.

Therefore most wooden workers would never use it to create furniture instead of choosing to work with real wood. While it is never the first choice for fine woodwork, OSB can certainly be useful and cost-effective for several utility applications.

OSB is not be for external use. These boards begin to break down after long exposure to the outside elements.

Pine

Pine has many practical uses and it is a very popular and versatile softwood. Pine is usually considered economical and sustainable making it a common option for a variety of projects.

Many pine trees grow very high and strong and are mostly grown in sustainable forestry conditions, which ensures that more trees are planted than ever in any given year.

There are many pine types with various characteristics. As the name suggests, Southern Yellow pine can have a yellower hue than the white or sugar pine varieties. White pine and sugar pine are also called transparent pine occasionally.

You may determine with pine whether to dye, paint or simply finish it with a clear protective sealant. Pine is perfect for staining a wide range of colours and shades if you prepare the wood well in advance.

Many pines are ideally suited for indoor use even if explicitly treated for outdoor use, as for the lumber handled under pressure that is also included in this list of wood types.

Plywood

Plywood is a wood product, not made of real wood, it is rendered by fastening and compressing several layers of the furnace together.

It can be made from a variety of different wood finishes, most of which have a "strong" and a "bad" face.

Plywood comes in various thicknesses: the quarter inch, the half-inch and the three-quarter-inch sizes are most likely to be seen in home improvement shops. The most widely used plate is made of fir, pine, or spruce in construction.

Pressure Treated Lumber

Pressure-treated wood is a traditional Southern Pine yellow wood, which is chemical resistant to red and pest. Some pressure-treated wood is often made of SPF wood, a generic Spruce, Pine & Fir acronym.

Pressure-treated wood is also used to create decks, patios, railings, and other exterior structures. Owing to the resistance of red lumber treated with pressure, it is also possible to salvage old wood treated with pressure to be used for new building projects.

When you plan to use pressurized wood in your designs, make sure you use fresh wood or wood imported after 2005.

Lumber treated with pressure was commonly harmful, containing some poisonous heavy metals such as arsenic. Fortunately, today's wood is much healthier, even though it is commonly recommended to be used only for products which are not in contact with food. There is a considerable debate as to whether lumber treated with pressure is healthy to use in raised garden beds used for food production.

Poplar

Poplar is a common and cost-effective hardwood used for building projects and applications. The colour of the wood is very soft and can even look white. It does not necessarily have a distinctive or appealing wood grain, so poplar is often painted or used where it is not visible.

Poplar is softwood, making it easy to work with, but it can also be very easy to break and knock when working with it.

This wood is less likely to warp or shift. Since it is not necessarily the most beautiful wood, it is mostly used in pieces of furniture that are not visible, such as drawers and the inside parts of dresser frames.

It is most frequently used in templates as well as in other woodworking applications. It is available readily at most stores which sell wood and in smaller parts at hobby stores and artisan stores which sell it for craft projects.

Rosewood

Rosewood is music for the ears of a woodworker; this wood used most frequently for guitar, piano and other wood instrument.

Rosewood is an exotic hardwood that often adds to common musical instruments' high prices. Brazilian rosewood is common, but it may come from Madagascar or Asia as well. Many people are worried about illegal logging and deforestation, so they prefer to choose alternate forests for their projects.

This type of wood is also a known irritant to many, particularly with prolonged sawdust exposure that may occur when the wood is cut. If you are working with rosewood, the appropriate wood safety precautions are extremely important.

SPF Lumber

SPF timber is not a particular wood type; it's a common word that includes Spruce, Pine and Fir, which is how the SPF acronym is used and recognized.

All these trees are softwoods with similar characteristics and properties, but the eye has significant variations.

SPF wood is most widely used for interior design and utility purposes. Since it is a commodity, sometimes the type of wood that you get as an SPF depends mostly on current supply and demand conditions.

SPF is also used for utility or interior walls framing. The wood cannot normally withstand harsh environmental conditions unless it is chemically altered and under strain.

Its wood can normally be sanded to be painted easily but is generally not suitable for colouration because of the growing block ability.

SPF lumber is generally very inexpensive, but often costs more when you attempt to use it for finer woodworking projects, especially if you take a lot of time to make the wood usable for what you want to create.

It is also important to buy SPF lumber at the same time, as this increases the probability that at least all the wood you are buying will be the same species and share the same characteristics.

If you deal with SPF woodworking, you will want to buy more than you think you need, simply because it can be volatile from time to time.

It is also necessary to ensure that you have time to acclimatize the humidity and temperature of your shopping to prevent severe shrinking and swelling during cuts and projects.

Spruce

Spruce is an evergreen softwood tree, and as described above, "SPF lumber," mostly used for construction framing, can be found in wooden yards.

Spruce has a rather light colour, and often it is also sold under the "White Wood" generic umbrella, particularly in large housing retail chains. It has got a simple, subtle kernel.

When spruce can grow to its highest maturity, it can have excellent acoustic characteristics which make it desirable for the construction of musical instruments like piano and guitar.

Spruce was used historically for the building of aircraft and warships. The first aircraft designed by the Wright Brothers was made from Spruce. Nevertheless, spruce is susceptible to swelling and not particularly resistant to the heat, so it is no longer usually used for such applications.

Teak

Teak is an exotic hardwood from the rainforests of Asia. It takes a very long cycle of growth, and the average tree takes 60 years to harvest.

While today more sustainable forestry practices have been in place than there have been decades ago, teak is still a hardwood to find at a very high price.

It is the most widely used for boat building and it's still a favourite among nautical artisans and craftspeople. In premium outdoor furniture, decks and other outdoor applications, it is also very popular.

Teak has a naturally oily finish, which can sometimes make it difficult to stain or glue. The wood is also quite difficult, and so you can notice that when you work with it, you need to sharpen and replace your blades more often.

Teak has an aroma that would be described by many as very distinct and terrestrial. Some people may be extremely sensitive to the natural oils in teak wood, and therefore it is necessary not to use teak for any application that has long and direct contact with food or skin.

It is also wise to use a dust respirator and gloves when working with teak. This helps to reduce your irritation while working with the wood. In case of allergy or allergies, it is best to avoid teak and to choose a more hypoallergenic wood for your designs.

Walnut

Walnut is a hardwood best known for its rich dark brown colour. It can be pricey and mostly only available in specialist woodworking shops, but for special projects, it is a beautiful choice.

Walnut is relatively easy but also very strong to work with. It can be used on hardwood floors, but many people still choose maple or white oak and stain the wood to match the desired shade of the walnut, because it is slightly longer lasting.

Walnut is a fine seed wood that polishes well and can be stained and protected easily. For carving, routing and decorative accents, many people like to use it for wood furniture. Walnut cabinets are very popular, though less expensive woods are commonly stained in the walnut colour.

Many people are also surprised to learn that walnuts are used in the production and construction of high-end luxury cars. The fibres of the walnut are very thick so that the wood can withstand the shock and strength in these uses.

It can also usually be made from musical instruments such as guitars and violins. While walnut is one of the expensive hardwoods, it is still much more economical to transform than other exotic hardwoods.

Whitewood

"Whitewood" is not a particular wood species and has not a form, but it's a common term for a wide variety of woods which have similar strength and color characteristics.

Whitewood is the word, the largest retail shops use and is used to refer to a single SKU number for a set of different trees, depending on their availability. Often this wood may be Cedar, Poplar, or Douglas fir.

Basically, if anything is sold as "whitewood," you generally don't know what kind of wood you might get. This wood form is sometimes sold as dimensional wood and is used in building and framing projects.

If you to identify different species of wood, sometimes in the generic "whitewood" section you will find great deals with woods like poplar and pine, but you also need to be careful because sometimes smaller grades are also marketed as whitewood.

Whitewood is basically the 'chocolate box' in the wood world – you don't know what you will get.

Zebrawood

Last but not least, the rare wood is known as Zebrawood. There are several Zebrawood varieties, most of them from Central America and Central Africa.

This wood is characterized by its distinctive pattern in the grain of the wood. It is most used for luxury furniture because of the simplicity of its distinctive design. It is a very thick, rough wood that can be hard to deal with sometimes.

Zebrawood has traditionally been used most commonly in high-end luxury products. The density and hardness make it desirable to be manufactured in things such as automobiles, weapons and other products which require shock and vibration.

This is today most used as a wood veneer used to give decorative accents to different pieces of furniture. There is a great deal of concern about the safe and legal harvesting of this exotic wood, and you may want to consider other hardwood alternatives to ensure that your projects are environmentally friendly.

There is the right type of wood for you, whatever you want to create.

Now that we've researched the different wood types and discussed many of their common uses and features, hopefully, it will be much easier for you to select the right wood for your project.

Whether you create indoors or outdoors, whether you decide to make a simple shelf or carve a complex piece of art, there is always the perfect wood for your project!

MUST-HAVE TOOLS FOR WOODWORKING

Woodwork means different things for different people. Many woodworkers create useful and robust components to relieve tension and exercise their imaginative muscles. They are enthusiastic people who know that sawdust is good for the soul. Others are becoming professionals. They are well balanced for skills in constructing suitable furniture. But no matter whether they are master craftsmen or amateur rank, you need the necessary woodwork tools. For knowledge on these devices, read this entire guide. In short, the required woodworking tools include the following:

- Power saws
- Hand saws
- Planes
- Sanders
- Files

- Hammer
- Mallet
- Drill
- Screw Gun
- Tape Measure
- Square
- Sawhorses
- Workbench

Most beginning woodworkers are frustrated by the large variety of resources on the market. It's convenient for them to bring in their company tens of thousands of dollars of expensive woodworking equipment. Nonetheless, most tools for beginner woodworkers don't have to be complicated and costly. The woodworking tools of beginners will start with the basics to give a sense of simplicity that is the essence of great work.

Five levels of basic woodworking tools are available. These are devices for cutting, wrapping, assembling, measuring, and carrying wooden pieces and turning raw materials into projects. Such tool classes cover all a woodworker requires to create simple to complex objects. To help you decide what should be included in your simple toolbox, here is a guide for beginners who need woodworking equipment.

SAWS USED FOR WOODWORKING

Nearly every aspect of a woodworking project begins with material cutting. The best and most interesting pieces begin with rough wood lengths. If it is hardwood like oak or softwood like pine, a wood stock must be ribbed and cut to form. Saws are the solution, but they come in different types and sizes. These are also ideal for different cutting tasks. This is what you need to start creating your saws' set.

CIRCULAR SAW

If there's one power-activated saw belonging in every beginner's box, it's a circular saw. There are endless brands available, but they all have a common feature: a round or circular blade full of sharp teeth that tear through the wood. All circular saws are electric, although they come in different power ratings. Most are corded tools running on household current, but there have been great advances in cordless circular saws.

Some people see circular saws as more ideal for rough carpentry than for fine woodworking. That's not true at all. In the other hand, circular saws cut straight, clean lines. A lot depends on the blade you use.

Circular saw blades come in three types:

Blades: Cut the material along the length or with the grain

Blades: for sifting through the grain

Combination blades: For ribbing and cross-cutting.

The distinction between blades is the nature of their teeth. Ribblades have uniformly spaced teeth, while transverse blades have staggered teeth. The blades have all tooth styles. If budget is your issue, it is best to invest in a good carbide-fitted blade. Additionally, blade diameters must be known.

Circular saws in two distinct designs are available. Firstly, the blade is mounted 90 degrees directly on the engine and on the harbour. Direct drives are the most common and least expensive circular saws. Worn circular drive saws are designed for heavy work. They still have the same blade designs, but the blade is ahead of the piston.

JIGSAW

Each woodworker from the beginning should invest in a decent puzzle. Saben saws are often referred to as their identical, sabre-like comb. Such power tools are built to make complex, smooth, curved, or serpentine cuts. Think of the lines in a puzzle, and you are going to realize what a puzzle can be.

Jigsaws are totally different from circular saws. Because of spinning blades, jigsaws cut back and forth or up and down. In tooth numbers and shape, blades differ. They are used for cutting metal, plastic and wood. Fine dental blades are used for veneer sawing, while coarse dental blades are used for fast and rough work.

Jigsaws with one hand is easy to control and you should keep your job tightly with the other hand. Jigsaws can beautifully cut tiny, complicated pieces. Inner cuts such as the inner circle or triangle are one of the best uses for a puzzle. You just drill a pilot hole and put the blade in. You will soon learn to make plunge cuts with your jigsaw with some practice.

COMPOUND MITER SAW

Compound miter saws are a change from standard circular saws. They have the same snap, cross-cut and blades as circular saws. These are therefore mounted in an arm or track close to the radial arm saws that they have nearly replaced. The diameters of the common blades are 10 and 12 inches, but compound miter saws can be mounted to a smaller size of 7 1/2. For a miter saw, a standard cross-section saw blade should always be used.

These electric saws are highly flexible instruments. For most shops, they have updated the traditional miter box and backsaw. Beginners find that powerful miter-saws produce much more precise cuts for miters, bevels, and compound angles. It is easy to set at 22 1/22, 45 and 90 ° standard angles, but it can be adjusted for any angle between them. It requires right and left cuts.

Powered miter saws were developed by the standard cut-off and chop saw. They are now available in sliding-armed versions that increase the cutting range. Their powerheads tilt to each side so that the miters and bevel cuts can be combined. Using a compound miter saw, virtually, any set of angles can be removed.

TABLE SAW

Earlier in the game, most first woodworkers invested in a table saw. Table saws produce cuts which are not easy to achieve with other forms of saws. They are shaped like circular saws upside-down in which the blade from below the table saw or the working surface is exposed. Blade depth and angle can be changed easily for accuracy.

There are three models of table saws and they are ideal for beginners. It depends on the scale of the job: you may want a fixed table saw to stay in a shop or a portable saw to take away. Those are your options at the table:

The table saws on the cabinet are heavy and made to stay in place. Their name comes from the fact that their motors are in a lower armchair with a blade operated by a pulley and belt system. Those are great for all-round work, from wood-rubbing to panel cutting. Many beginners choose a table as the centrepiece of their laboratory.

The table saws on benchtop are lighter duty. They are designed to be compact so that they can be suitable both to travel and to store. Most benchtop table saws are direct drive. Direct drive helps them to be compact, but they continue to be noisy.

The tightest prototypes are the contractor table saws. Building contractors prefer them to cut quickly and conveniently at areas where time and space are premium. Contractor table saws are often cost-effective and a good option for beginners to learn about their work.

A quality blade should always be used to make a table saw, also known as a chop saw or chop box, such as carbide tip blades or rip scroll blade.

Bandsaw

There is nothing like a bandsaw to tear raw material or make complex curved cuts. Such power supplies are a mixture of circular and sabre-saws that connect the teeth to a constantly looped flat steel strip that rotates around the top and bottom pulleys. There is a flat table between the sleeves that tilts for angled cuts.

Depending on the size of the stock you cut and how complicated you want your cuts to be, there are two key features of band saws, each deciding the choice of a band saw size:

Depth capability is the extent to which the blade between the pulleys is exposed. It is also known as a face gap, ranging from 4 "to 12" or more for small bandsaws for large machinery. This defines the thickness of your material ability.

Throat depth measures from the teeth of the blade to the back of the frame of the support. This determines the size of your stock. A deep throat capability makes angled cuts where work needs to be placed on the table simpler.

The coarse teeth for quick cuts and fine teeth for a smooth, slower cut are accessible. With bandsaws, blade width is critical. Big blades are more secure for slicing, whereas thin blades simplify curved cutting.

Be sure to invest in standard band saws' tires for a better use.

Handsaws

Every woodworker's shop always has a place for handsaws. Handsaws are so easy and quick to use for required and detailed precision cuts. There is no bulky weight, tormented cords or batteries that die nice with handsaws. Handsaws are also still set and not expensive to go.

They have been around for centuries. These are essentially a steel blade with a wooden handle to move the job back and forth. But the handsaw application is far more than most beginners think.

Some handsaw designs to consider:

Handsaws ripping: Cut with wood grain

Handsaws cross-cut: Work into the wood grain

Handsaws combination: Can be used for both rips and crosscuts

Backsaws: Use rectangular blades for miter cutting with braced back.

Carcase Handsaws: Longer and heavier hands

Handsaws Coping: Like jigsaws and angled cutting bandsaws

Dovetail handsaws: Joint work for fine dovetail

Handsaws Keyhole: Made to cut inner holes

Beginning woodworkers should invest in handsaws of the best quality possible. The most frustrations are from cheap or dull blades. A sharp blade with excellent teeth is almost as fast and true to wood as an electric screw.

FILING, PLANING, AND SANDING SUPPLIES USED IN WOODWORKING

Once wood parts are cut to a rough form, they require further work to produce an appealing, finished look. No matter how good your piece is, some kind of filing, planning and sanding supplies are always required. Here are what great woodworkers also consider:

Planes

Planes are cutting machines usually used instead of abrasive sanding machines. All types of planes use a fixed blade to shave wood fibres and make them smoother. The key factors are blade size, and depth and how much material can be withdrawn at a time.

You 're going to learn some plane names that sound a little strange or humorous. Rabbet planes and jack planes both shave wood but vary considerably. You can also hear words like jointers, spokeshaves and lines. You will get to know them by numbers too. Here are all sorts of hand planes to be explored by beginning woodworkers:

Jack Plane: This instrument extracts a great deal of material in a run. It's a tool for the "jack of all-round" because it's available for smoothing or jointing both curved and straight edge types.

Block planes: These are smaller and more powerful planes. They are ideal for tight work where very smooth joints are required.

Joining planes: Like jack planes, except for smooth edges and joined parts. Jointers typically have long frames.

Rabbet Planes: Used to trim right corner grooves along the edge of the grained plate. Such joints are known as rabbits, which differ from the so-called dados within grooves.

Scraper planes: Designed to remove fine fibres from wood surfaces to make them super smooth. These aircraft are sometimes referred to as scraper cabinets.

Spokeshaves: hand planes for curved surfaces. They were initially for wheel spokes but made their way to all woodworkers.

Orbital Sander

If one electric wood finishing tool is going to be bought, it should be an orbital sander. Such fast-acting devices strip all pressure from hand sanding and do it much faster. Orbital sanders vary from inline instruments such as belt sanders. You use sandpaper pads that rotate in a circular or orbital pattern.

Standard orbital sanders take and turn into a circle the circular abrasive sandpaper disk. However, if they remove material easily, they appear to leave swirl marks that are difficult to remove. Your next buy is a random orbital sander. Alternatively, they spontaneously oscillate, leaving the wood surface silky and mark-free.

Hand Files

There is often no better tool than a smooth and even wood file. Hand files are cheap and last a long time when you buy the quality steel files ones. Once dull, the best way to replace hand files is to sharpen them. Here are your key choices of hand files:

Rasps are instruments with rough teeth. They are used for removing large quantities of wood for general forming and then allow finer files to take over.

Half-round files on one side have a flat surface and on the other a curved lip. This makes it possible to work on straight and curved surfaces.

Mill files on both sides are square. Usually, they have rough teeth on one side, and they are fine on the other. Those also have close room toothed edges.

Rotary cutters are like papers, except for electric drill bits. You put them in your boiler chuck and extract material from the rotary abrasive action. Rotary files in different patterns and grit cutting are disponible.

Generally, metal files are made of high-grade steel and have exceptionally fine teeth. As with any device, you typically get what you pay for but investing in high-quality hand files is worth it.

ASSEMBLY TOOLS FOR WOODWORKING

Woodcuts and smoothes are just part of your whole woodworking process. When the parts are substantial and smooth enough to finish, they just do need to be assembled. Successful assembly of woodwork relies on two issues: you need correct joints that match and you also need the right equipment to connect and mount them properly.

What are the basic assembly methods for newcomers?

HAMMER

There is no universal woodworking hammer. Maybe a carpenter's claw hammer is as close to a single-size tool, but there are also several dozen different types of hammering. Woodworking hammers usually have two tasks to perform and these are pounding and pries. How well they do that depends on a few things:

Head style with facial size and weight. Many heads are flat, like hammers. Some have clamping faces for clamping nails and fasteners, as seen in hammers for framing.

Claw design including curve and weight. Hammers with long and strong claws use a straighter edge to divide materials while framing tools.

The composition of the handle is critical for comfort. Most of first woodworkers prefer a hammer handle of wood or composite because these shock less when they are striking. But framers like handles of steel. Further shock is induced, but steel adds weight and there's more driving force. Steel handles don't easily break, too.

Weight overall is significant. The weight of the hammer is measured in ounces. Hammers are 8 to 10 ounces lightweight. The intermediate hammer's weight between 16 and 20 oz, while heavy hammers weight between 24 and 32 oz.

The purpose and composition of hammers differ. Newcomers in woodworking have a range of options but they need to decide what their hammers should be for before they buy. Here are the major types of hammers for woodwork:

Hammers are all-intentional. This will be your first purchase because it is so easy.

Hammers for framing are difficult. But, for most projects, they are a little overcrowded.

Hammers of tack are like brad horses. They are for small jobs and usually have two heads with no claws.

MALLET

Do not combine branches with hammers. Both are striking devices, but their implementations are entirely diverse. Hammers are usually made of steel, but some of them are made of brass or plastic. While mallets have large heads of wood or leather and detachable handles to accommodate different head sizes.

The difference is their striking surprise and impression of the air. Mallets are much smaller than hammers and rather than produce shock absorption. These also leave minimal striking marks and make suitcases ideal for tapping together wood joints.

Starting carpentry, you should know that you never use a hammer in steel on chisels. The steel hammers shock causes the chisels to stab or jab on the wood, leaving raw finishes. Nevertheless, tapping chisels in a briefcase lets them slice effortlessly with steady pressure through the wood.

POWER DRILL

Power drill can be the best friend of beginner woodworkers. Only a few old craftsmen still use a brace and a little or a hand drill. Electric boxes are used for many purposes in the laboratory, so it is not just for boiling holes. To turn your electric drill into other tools, you can buy all sorts of attachments.

If you buy your first power box, you must consider seriously obtaining a cabled model. Drills with 110/120 volt currents have much greater torque and endurance than cableless drills. Some can feel the cords get in the way, but they never leave you with a heavy load.

If you prefer wireless power boxes, the voltage is rated. Early models were 7.5-volt but were upgraded quickly. Even for beginners, 18-volt cordless drills are a good choice. They are not much more costly than 14-volt drills and have much more power.

Power drills may also be graded as chucks — 3/8 "chucks are the typical medium-size and 1/2." Drills can be found in keyless versions or chucks that simplify bit adjustments.

SCREW GUN

Screws are the best woodwork fasteners all around. They hold tight and can be removed when they are disassembled, temporary joints or errors occur. Of course, you do not want to be out of your normal hand screwdrivers but investing in a reliable screw gun makes turning screws quicker and easier. Screw guns are particularly valuable for multiple screw jobs.

Screw pistols are extensions of the family of power boxes. Most of the screw-guns are now cordless and comfortable. The principal difference between a real screw gun and a power box is the chuck 's interior shape. Screw arms are intended for inserting hexagonal or six-sided bit shanks. This means that slippage does not exist.

TOOLS FOR MEASUREMENT AND ANGLES

Twice they say weigh and once cut: the old woodworker's advice is the best. Any other advice is to purchase high quality, reliable and readable measuring equipment. Below you can find the key calculation and angle control devices you need as a carpenter:

SQUARES

Without a range of squares, it is highly impossible to build good wood projects. Great squares allow you to create and check all kinds of angles. Most squares do have on their surface gravure markings and this helps them to act as laws of measurement. Here are the ones you may want to have:

Framing Squares: large, rectangular tools for larger surfaces

Try Squares: Smaller, right-angle devices for quick squareness verification

Combination squares: used for correcting angles and distance

Speed Squares: allow you to check angles of 90 and 45 degrees quickly

Mitre squares: Best for setting angling miter cuts

Bevel Squares: Allow the development of an existing angle and transfer pattern

Technically, lines, compasses and depth measurements are not circles but are basic and invaluable devices for woodwork. They join the other family of tapes and rules.

TAPE MEASURES

At least one tape measure should be put on any woodworker's belt.

It would be difficult to add all the tape measures to your belt, however, since so many styles exist. These are the basic tapes to be taken into account:

Retractable steel tapes: these are the most common instruments of measurement. They are 12 to 30 feet tall.

Flexible bobbin tapes: you can get them in cotton or steel over 100 feet in lengths.

Folding Rulers: Note that rulers are not named. They are rigid sticks with high precision calculation. Some rulers are divided into many parts.

Yardsticks and Straight Edges: they are in the ruler family, and they are useful for quick and straight lines.

OTHER NECESSITIES FOR SUCCESSFUL WOODWORKING PROJECTS

Now that you have an idea of what are the beginning tools to cut, finish, assemble and measure woodwork projects, you need a way to keep them ongoing. Clamping equipment in woodworking shops is important. Sawdust and your standard workbench are the two best keeping tools:

SAWHORSES

Sawhorses are one of the first investments that you should make as a joiner. They are simple four-legged as animals which balance well and support long lengths of wood and heavyweights. The sawdust is typically used in pairs, but a half dozen sawdust is known by many woodworkers.

You can make your own rigid wood sawdust. Using recycled materials is an economical way. But there are also many industrial sawdust items made of steel, fibreglass and plastic. Usually producing sawmills does not worth your time unless you want to do so.

QUALITY WORKBENCH

There is one real cost to remember as a first carpenter: a standard workbench.

Yeah, you can make your own out of 2x4s and plywood, but you will never get the utility of a high-quality skilled workbench that you 're going to use it all the time for every project. Here are several features to consider in a workbench of quality:

- Solid, hardwood construction
- Adjustable base for accurate levelling
- Two various sized vices
- Large working surface with built-in stops
- Lower drawers for storing tools
- Free-standing with 360-degree access

Repair and Maintenance of Woodwork Tools

Great woodworking tools are an important equipment that enables carpenters and other woodworkers to do woodworking in an effective and efficient manner. Nevertheless, the quality of broad woodworking can only be achieved if these fools are preserved and repaired according to schedule. Here is a list of the repair techniques you can use in your laboratory.

Regular Sharpening

Wooden chisels are some of the large carpentry instruments that need regular sharpening. Many woodworking tools are used to cut or boil wood, meaning they must be sharp enough to serve their tasks in keeping with the standards. If you want to improve your work by using your drilling and cutting equipment, you must ensure that a specialist regularly sharpens them.

Cleaning After Use

One of the primary methods to maintain your woodwork production constant is to clean your tools after you have used them. Dirt, mud and other debris could be the reason your woodworking instruments don't cut or boil holes as expected. Until your store, all the devices should be thoroughly washed and wiped-dry.

Drying Tools After Use

You will possibly operate on a wet or damp environment with your devices. You have to ensure that all moisture is washed out before storing them so that the devices are going to be dry. It prevents rust that is reused to a greater degree by a moist environment. Rusting causes us to wear and tear most woodwork tools within a shod era.

Oiling or Greasing

To reduce or remove the friction that causes wear and tear, rotting woodwork tools should be frequently grated. Your tools will be quiet, which means that your woodwork activities are less energy-efficient. Oiling is also a critical component of rust protection, which causes severe woodwork tools corrosion.

Repairing or Replacing Handles

Most woodwork instruments are handheld, which allows the handle to wear and to tear after a longer period. Acting with an unhandled tool causes blisters and pain in your palms. You need to make sure that worn-out handles are regularly repaired and replaced to avoid this issue.

As an expert carpenter, you want your woodworking equipment to be productive and at the right price. However, your woodworking tools can only produce optimum results by ensuring that they are regularly repaired and maintained.

GUIDE TO BUYING LUMBER FOR WOODWORKING

You have your new equipment, and you have found the ideal woodwork plans for DIY. But now you're on the island with all the wood choices.

Do you know what to buy for your project? How can the best boards be chosen? Why are certain boards more expensive than others?

Don't worry; I was there as well. When you first start working with wood, there is so much that you don't know, and that's fine. The lumber purchasing guide for newcomers helps you perfectly continue your woodwork journey.

WHY IS THE ACTUAL SIZE OF THE BOARD DIFFERENT THAN THE STATED SIZE?

If you look at woodworking plans or the store, you see the lumber by depth and width (for example 1 lumber 3, 2 lumber 4, 1 lumber8, etc.). If you measure the boards, however, you'll see that the lumber isn't the same size. This is what is known as dimensional wood.

This wood is cut to size and sawn and planned to make straight. The actual size of the board is, therefore, less than the specified (nominal) size.

Therefore, if your plans call for a 1/4 frame, the actual size is x 3 1/2″. And I wish I could assume that the real board size was always X smaller than the nominal size, but clearly, it is not.

I have made this useful map instead, to help you select the regular wood sizes. It should also be remembered that the dimensional measurement is only for the width and depth of the wood. The actual length is mentioned.

Lumber size cheat

Normal size	Actual size

1x1	¾ x ¾
1x2	¾ x 1 ½
1x3	¾ x 2 ½
1x4	¾ x 3 ½
1x6	¾ x 5 ½
1x8	¾ x 7 ¼
1x10	¾ x 9 ¼
1x12	¾ 11 ¼
2x2	1 ½ x 1 ½
2x3	1 ½ x 2 ½
2x4	1 ½ x 3 ½
2x6	1 ½ x 5 ½
2x8	1 ½ x 7 ¼
2x10	1 ½ x 9 ¼
2x12	1 ½ x 11 ¼

WHAT KIND OF WOOD SHOULD YOU BUY FOR YOUR PROJECT?

There are so many types of wood. And some are cheaper than others. So it is important to know what kind of wood works for your project so you don't waste time and money dealing with the wrong one.

You'll probably see very cheap fuzzy panels, more expensive typical boards, pricier select pine boards, and very expensive hardwood boards when you visit your nearest big box home improvement store.

Then, of course, there are outdoor wood choices such as redwood, cedar and pressurized boards. What does anything of all of this mean?

Furring strips

They are very appealing due to their cheapness especially if you are looking for low-cost wood. However, you can know the reason of their accessible price when you start digging through the surfaces.

Furring strips are also very rough, with plenty of imperfections and distortions. They are built for constructing and to lift or level items, but they are not meant to be used.

However, I've successfully used them in woodwork (I made the frames of the cabinet doors with 1 to 3 furring strips), but you need be able to pick up your boards and sand them with more time implication.

Framing lumber and studs

Framing wood is 2x4s (and 2x boards) used to frame a building. Such boards are inexpensive. The cheapest choice for stubs is made of whitewood (typically Douglas fir).

When you add a wall to your house, it is very likely that you will use it. Most woodworking plans use 2x4s online, and I really love to use them.

The foundation of our outdoor dining table, the slatted outdoor couch structure and the legs of the tiled tub benches were all made up of 2x studs.

The first big downside of 2x bolts is their rounded bottom. You can make these boards square by putting them through a table saw to eliminate the rounding (but by doing so you can also make the board smaller).

Common boards

Such boards are a great choice for beginners because they are very economical in addition to be straighter and prettier than the furring plates.

Popular panels are typically made of pine and are treated like softwood. For many woodworking projects, I use these boards with great results.

I have also used them for outdoor designs, such as the kid's patio furniture, the treasure-chest toy box and the water-like picnic table.

Common boards do not typically come in sizes 1 to 2 and 1 to 3 (start at 1 to 4 and expand from there). So, you can pull down boards with a table screw or circular screw, but also with a guide track if you need to obtain the wood even smaller.

Select pine boards

Such boards are a perfect way to keep a budget under control but still offer you great results. The pine boards are the crop's milk. They are often very straight (but always test your wood before buying) and only have few imperfections.

Choosing pine is my latest preference for my woodworking ventures. I can make pieces of furniture that are cheap but look fantastic: my sliding barn doors and console table were built with selected pines, and you can tell the difference.

Hardwood boards

In the home improvement store, Hardwood is probably the most expensive wood choice. There are several different hardwood types (walnut, cherry, and oak). These boards are usually sold by the linear foot, so make sure you look at a hardwood option carefully.

I wouldn't recommend these for beginner carpentry projects because you are going to make mistakes and these mistakes can be expensive for $4 + foot.

Yet hardwoods will give you amazing results. But first, know what you do, then create your heirloom with these amazing pieces.

For smaller plans, I enjoy using hardwood. Without a high-end price, it gives the high-end performance. They are also required to make cutting boards such as a handmade marble cheese board.

I recommend knotty alder if you want to get tougher wood on a budget. The knots give it the rustic quality, and the price of other hardwoods is around 1/2. This is what we used to do when we opened our mission-style shelf vanity to hold a bathroom to use and to keep it moist.

Poplar is another great budget-friendly choice. That is what I used for our kitchen remodeling cabinet doors and hands. The furniture is very popular because it can have a slight green undertone, but I used it with stain and I loved it.

Pressure-treated lumber

Pressure-treated wood is your framing wood which is treated to withstand ends, red and fungal decline. This is used for ground touch and for decks. We used it in our outdoor playhouse deck and in our pergola patio.

Redwood and cedar can also be used for outdoor ventures. Naturally, they are immune to decay and materials, but they have a much higher price.

Plywood

Plywood is a great woodworking choice. It's simple, inexpensive and can be of any size you like for your project.

Plywood is a thin layer of hardwood over a pressed wood and glue sandwich. It provides a solid wood with a good stain or paint coat.

The edges of the splayed wood are normally hidden, but I occasionally like to expose them for an industrial look (as I did with our splayed closet organizer).

Plywood is priced dense. Yet 1/4" plywood is not 1/4" necessarily. It is more of an inch 7/32. It extends to all splintering thicknesses. Check the actual product thickness before purchasing it.

Plywood is typically sold in sheets of 4'x8" and 2'x4". I almost never buy 2'x4' sheets since they cost roughly 1/4 of the total 4'x8' sheets and because the plate is so flexible.

Most beginners are remaining outside of the plateau because they think they need a table saw to cut it. So, you can receive a few free cuts from the home improvement store or use inexpensive equipment such as a circular saw to cut it.

HOW DO YOU CHOOSE STRAIGHT BOARDS?

If you know what wood you want to purchase, the straightest boards you can purchase are imperative. Curves and warps on the boards cause the woodworking loads of pain and tension.

Take the extra time at the store to check each board before you buy it.

To test if a board is straight, hold it up to your nose and look down at the board length, then you will see if the surface is curving or turning.

Flip the board 1/4 if it looks straight and looks down to the next page. Turn the board 1/4 and test the board's four sides straight before choosing the board.

Examine the breaks, knots and other imperfections of the entire board. Knots are always perfect for your woodworking project to add dimension, but knots are super hard and can be broken out of boards by cutting or drilling.

You may need additional wood to ensure that the cuts do not pass through knots. Stop buying broken frames.

HOW TO STORE BOARDS TO MINIMIZE WARPING

After you've bought the right boards, take them home and store them correctly to keep them straight.

Hang boards flat on the floor or on racks covering the entire board width.

Stack boards so that they are straight and smooth.

Boards will bend or twist from improper storage (and it can occur rapidly if the air is very moist).

Woodworking Measuring and Marking-Out Guide

Measurement and recognition are vital parts of every realistic project. Planning should help ensure that the project works and reduce the risk of mistakes and waste.

If two pieces of wood with high-quality clamps are glued together, the link between them is stronger than the wood itself. But you need to learn how to measure, mark, and precisely cut wood every time, before you can take out the power instruments and begin the assembly of your woodworking projects. Since the glue bond isn't as solid as it should be, only one piece of paper will fit between two pieces of joined wood.

In addition to helping to create good connections and even touch, taking the time to cut every piece of your project correctly can help to get it together as you planned with minimal time spent on sanding or correcting. It is true that not every cut is vital to the success of the job in certain instances. Yet it cannot hurt to be just as accurate as possible, and to be consistent helps to develop healthy habits.

The aim is to prepare the materials for the next phases of the production cycle. If materials are incorrectly measured and labelled, they can result in joints not matching or incorrectly aligned and connected.

There are several key points for proper calculation and marking:

- reading the proportions of the sketches or drawings, accurately.
- Choose the best equipment and material for your mission.
- To correctly and properly use devices.
- Test the calculation and test it for accuracy.
-

MARKING-OUT TOOLS

Woods

The following instruments are commonly used for wood measurement and marking:

Pencil – used for marking lines and centres to be cut or joined. Afterwards, pencil marks are easy to erase. A sharp pencil can be used very gently. This gives the workpiece thin, light lines that do not grave.

Steel rulers – used to measure cutting or joining materials. Also used flat on the bottom and side tops. It means that measuring from a single consistent point is labelled.

Marking wood with steel and pencil can offer precise and removable markings.

Tripod – Used to draw perpendicular lines of materials, to mark the woodworking joints' sides. Better used against the side with the brass edge smooth. It makes sure the line is parallel.

Marking gage – used to write lines in parallel to the edges, to remove waste wood from the woodwork.

The marker must be flat on the side of the workpiece. You should not dig the spur into the material you want to cut and instead run it gently over several times until a torn-out line is scored on the wood. A marking measurement is used to write a line parallel to a surface.

Gage for cutting – Used to cut a wood line parallel to the edge, to mark a woodwork joint. The stock must be flat on the side of the piece. It is necessary to ensure that the tool is inserted and labelled into the workpiece.

Mortise gage – used to write a two-line parallel to an edge. When marking the workpiece, two sharp spurs should be balanced and matched to the width of the mortise chisel. The stock of the mortise gage must be flat on the piece side.

It is best not to dig the spur into the workpiece and run it carefully a few times before a scored line is formed between the two points.

Sliding bevel – Used to set an angle for cutting waste material or marking joints for woodwork. You can change the bevel blade to establish the exact angle. The lines on the material to be cut are then labelled with a pencil. This is used to set an angle.

MEASURING AND MARKING WOOD BEFORE CUTTING.

Measure, mark, cut, then. It sounds simple, right? Not exactly. Regardless of whether you use a ruler or a tape measurement, always double-check your measurements (or three times!). Make sure your wood is well numbered. A pencil works perfectly as a marker if the tip is sharp. And when accuracy is of utmost importance, make your mark with a razor blade or box cutter. This gives you the tightest possible precision and straightness for cutting. In addition, this small cut has the added benefit of lightening the wood grain slightly, which makes the wood less likely to split as you cut it.

You have three options to use if you use a pencil to make your mark before you cut the wood: you can cut it into the inside, along the lines or out of the line. For most cases, the cutting outside of the line is advised. You can always take more wood off, but once you've started cutting, you can't get it back. The blade of the saw will shift on the side of the wall. If you cut to the lines of crayon, your blade thickness could remove more material than you expected. Regardless of what you pick, always be sure to cut. Take the same method for any cut the project needs, and correct cuts will appear.

ESSENTIAL WOODWORKING CUTS YOU SHOULD KNOW.

Now that you are ready to cut your wood, let's take a look at when we use five big woodwork cuts.

Crosscut. Any cut that slices across the grain direction of the wood is a crosscut. Use a miter saw, or a table saw to make this cut with good results. A table saw will allow you to cut wider wood pieces. Avoid using a band saw, as the wood crossing on a blade is tougher and a band saw will burn out the wood's edges or cause rough cuts.

Rip cut. A rip cut is a cut following the course of the grain of the wood. Think of it as a separation of the wood. This cut is easy to make with most saws, and a table saw with rip fence is used by many professional joiners for consistent, repeatable results. But be careful when you are holding the wood. Never try to push a table with your hands through a table saw. Use a pushbutton to guide the piece forward. A decent miter saw can also be used for rip cuts with a wide blade and a sharp point.

Resawing. You cut the edges of the boards to make thinner boards when you resaw wood. This is an ideal way for turning thick pieces of wood into thinner furnishing or bookmaking plates. The best device for this technique is a finely balanced miter saw. Once your wood is resawed, you can run your boards through a wood floor to make sure the surfaces are flat.

Miter cut. The incision of a miter is made at an angle other than 90 degrees (that is not a square cut). It is typically a 45-degree woodcut and is used in the manufacture of boxes, frames and other structures. A miter saw is not necessarily the perfect method for miter cutting. A bevel cut is very similar to a miter cut except for the formation of angled or circular borders. Hold the face of the board against the fence of your miter sick to make bevel cuts. And to be secure, position the fence so that the blade tilts away.

Curved cut. Any cut that is intentionally not a straight cut is a curved cut. A band saw is suitable for curved cuts. Also, break out of your signature, so you have to round the edges separately. A puzzle can provide better results for thinner wood.

Woodworking Tricks and Tips for Beginners

I still look for shortcuts to save time or to make my life easier. Over time I have found a different way to do something that I have done a hundred times before, and I wonder why it was never easier for me to discover.

Below are ten woodworking tips that I have acquired from experts, or on my own. These tips are easy but effective ways to keep wood organized and functional.

Wood Layout - Triangle Registration

It's easy to mix wood pieces when you lay them, especially when you have several cuts of a similar length. Numbering the parts and where they join is fine, but using a triangular shape is even easier.

If the pieces are shifted, you can quickly visualize their position with each other, because only one way is to make the triangle shape together.

Set a triangle on your wood when it sits in the right position to ensure that part of the triangle hits all the pieces that you want to register. A straight edge makes this a quick and easy way to keep even the most complex adhesive references correctly.

Whether you have boards in a particular orientation laminated together or just multiple parts in a particular place, the triangle record mark is a great tool to use.

MARKING CUT LINES

I consider it helpful to place a little tick mark on the side when measuring material to be cut. This basic technique saves countless time and lets me calculate the thickness of the blade with which you cut.

Kerf is the difference between the left and right sides of the teeth of the saw and any cutting causes the loss of wood to become scrub. If you cut the blade kerf straight on the marked line through your measured object, it would be inaccurated. It may not sound like a big deal, but you know how frustrating it can be when you've ever had a 1/8 "job.

The answer is to measure the piece and make a small tick on one side of the measured line, indicating the side to be shaved. When measured, line the blade up to the line with your blade to be positioned on the ticked side, so that it is on one side of the line and not in the measured area.

STRAIGHT LINES ON DOWELS

Creating a line on a dowel is something that comes up all the time and can seem a difficult job, given all the fancy measuring tools you have. But the solution is simple: the dowel on any slotted surface. It is the track of your table saw in the workshop and can lay a pencil against the track and dowel for a line.

Have you not seen a table? Use any door jamb or box. This trick will work with all kinds of cylindrical artifacts that you like.

STORY STICK

Precise measurements are necessary, but repetitive measurements can easily be minimized by making a story stick, a measuring guide easily usable from any square scrap.

The stories are great because they can be as specific as you need, they are less burdensome than tape measurements, and there is no chance of a misread measurement after you have the measurement marked.

A story stick can also be used from drilling holes at a constant distance from the ground. Use a story stick as usual, but open the calculated mark this time. You can now use your story stick as a guide for drilling.

DRILL DEPTH

Not every hole boiled must be entirely through the stuff. While it's easy to set up stops on a drill press, it is quite often the best tool (portability, material size, etc.) to use the press. The development of a depth marker for a handheld power box is as simple as using a tape piece to show the desired depth.

GLUE CLEANUP

Glue is an excellent tool for many woodworking projects. The application of glue is easy, but a little mess can regularly occur. When the adhesive is still warm, cleaning the glue is as easy as spreading the sawdust on the adhesive and rubbing it around to remove the excess adhesive. This is a better way of extracting glue from a damp tissue or sponge because moisture can cause wood swelling.

Cleaning your hands is even easier. When your hands are covered, you can remove it quickly by just rubbing your hands together. The wet or still moist adhesive should flake off.

KEEP SLIPPERY GLUE-UPS STEADY

Not every glue job would go smoothly, and sometimes wood pieces are wanted to slip apart when being clamped together. This is especially true if you have multiple pieces that are being glued together and secured in a single clamp. An easy fix for this is sprinkling a small amount of salt onto the glue before clamping.

The salt crystal shape acts like square wheels on a car, preventing the pieces from sliding around.

When clamping the salt, it is embedded into the wood and is untraceable from the outside.

Wax Paper Cover

To glue your work to the bench accidentally is a mistake which normally only happens once. Keep your workbench clean by capturing glue drops, holding a roll of wax or parchment paper under your glue-up will also prevent you from grasping on the bench while drying

It is easier to unroll more wax paper than I feel I would need to cut it to the particular form while it's underworked, rather than to use the clamped edge on the roll. A shop ruler works very well to rub a clean edge on wax paper.

Hold Glue-Ups Instantly

Sometimes a pin doesn't fit into the part I have to glue, and sometimes I'm too eager to wait until the wood adhesive has been placed before I move into the next part of the build. For these situations, hot glue is a big crutch to use for wood.

Stick in your warm glue tool and let it exceed the temperature before applying some wood glue. Once your hot glue is ready, apply the wood glue as usual but always leave small gaps in the piece.

When the wood glue has been applied, apply a heat glue squirt to the wood glue gaps. Place the wood parts together and keep in place for a few seconds until the warm glue can be placed. The hot glue binds the two pieces to work and keeps the wood in place until the wood glue can hold and tie.

SANDPAPER ORGANIZATION

I have all sorts of abrasive paper on hand if I need a particular form. As such, my stock of sandpaper is a mess. Since practically all sandpapers are the same size as printer paper, I kccp them all in a cheap accordion-type file folder.

I pulled out the package with all my sandpaper and sorted it by grit. Every grate has its own folder slot, and the front pouch is reserved for smaller sandpaper scraps.

My sandpaper is all in one place, so I can simply pick up the folder and bring it back to my job.

WOOD GLUES

Enhance your woodworking skills by learning which adhesive form will work best for your project.

Wood earns praise for being a beautiful building material by its unique grain patterns and natural tones. And also for being relatively easy to construct with. The smooth, porous surface makes it easy to connect sections with nails or screws or with glue.

In addition, joining timber properly also requires a combination of fasteners – that is, a little wood glue between the pieces of timber is added before you screw them together to secure the connection.

Pay careful attention when you are planning your next woodworking or repair project, to the sort of wood glue to which you will use to obtain it. Each wood glue is not the same, so the best approach is to ensure the quality of finishing your wood and to achieve the strongest possible bonding. Please ask yourself these questions when considering your options:

Should you connect two surfaces or fill a gap?

Is the connection meant to last, or is it a temporary fix?

Does the attached or filled surfaces stay inside, or will the glue have to withstand external conditions?

Your requirements will allow you to choose the options that are ideally suited for your carpentry project.

Choosing the Right Type of Wood Glue

You can see very easily, when shopping for an adhesive, that there is not just one type of wood glue – instead, there are five wide varieties. Most wood glues are synthetic polymers or resins that are stronger than the wood itself, excluding hiding and animal collagen glues. In terms of bond toughness, strength, toxicity and waterproofness, these glues also vary in make-up (some can even affect the wood's finish more than others).

Polyvinyl Acetate (PVA) is a synthetic rubbery polymer that creates a permanent and flexible bond.

This wooden glue is non-toxic (except for the ingestion), water-soluble (thinned in small amounts of pure water) and suitable for a wide range of projects, particularly for wood- non-structural connections. White PVA varieties are for indoor use while yellow varieties are for outdoor use (also known as 'carpenter glue'). Check for "waterproof" on the label when you need a water-resistant glue.

PVA leaves a residue, affecting the finish of your wood – particularly oak. Another disadvantage is that PVA does not very well accept wood stain. It looks patchy when you try to stain the dried glue. Before it is dry, make sure you wipe away any excess glue with a Q-tip or sponge. Press the wood pieces with a clamp for best results until the glue is dry; if clamping is not practical, such as gluing a wood plug into a screw socket, apply a few minutes' pressure by hand. Then allow the flow of air (from an open window or fan) to create a strong link. Know that PVA glues are basically permanent; the adhesive can't be reversed or removed for repairs once it is dry.

Polyurethane is a synthetic plastic resin that creates solid, durable bonds.

Polyurethane is an important component in many wood types of glue, from paint to wood floor finishes. These wood glues arc excellent when joining wood grains — for instance when connecting two crown moulds — forming versatile and long-lasting joints. Polyurethane is moisture enabled, which means it relates to moisture in the air, meaning that, unlike other wood adhesives, it sticks very well and does not dry out sensitive wood fibres in wet conditions.

This toxic material must be treated carefully. Always remember to work in a well-ventilated room, wear a face mask and glass to prevent inhalation of glue fumes. If you want to stain your wood, you must know how easier polyurethane is than PVA. Nevertheless, remove excess glue with mineral spirits — water is not strong enough.

Cyanoacrylate (CA) is a fast-drying acrylic resin — and another superglue name.

Once broken, these bonds are extremely strong and rigid, which is beneficial if only a temporary bond must be formed — a few taps of a hammer or brush breaks it. CA glue may be used to attach glue blocks, or short wooden strips designed for refurbishment, to the back of a fresh furniture joint as long as it is required. It is also useful to fill cracks when mixed with sawdust.

CA glue does not bind to a dry wood surface and allows the wood to be slightly damp before use, as opposed to other wood glues. Nevertheless, it binds at room temperatures immediately and should be treated with care and precision. When working with runny, waterlike adhesive, wear a mask and protective gloves; remove the superglue with acetone (nail polish remover if any glue hits your skin). Acetone can be used to extract too much super glue from your working surface, but if not used properly, this chemical solvent can also weaken your timber finish. The short shelf-life means that CA glue works only on short-term projects.

Hide glue is the easiest alternative for restoring wood furniture.

Boiled animal collagen in nature, hide glue comes in two forms: liquid and solid crystals melted into a hot water bath and placed in a brush. The fluid hide glue (room temperature) uses urea crystal additives to preserve its fluidity and allows more time to work. By comparison, hot glue heals when it cools shortly after application. Today, woodworkers choose for their leeway (i.e. reversibility) both kinds of hiding glue, which they have when it dries. It produces durable but flexible joints – which is why many antiquities are still remedied with hiding glue. The use of this adhesive preserves the integrity of antique items and honours traditional craft.

In liquid form, hide glue helps you to match two pieces of wood perfectly. When fully set and dried, the furniture building and other strong and enduring bonds are an excellent choice. The two types of hiding glue are also used in the construction of guitars and stringed instruments. Best of all, it does not affect the finish of your wood.

Epoxy is the perfect wood filler to cover holes and cracks.

Like other wood glues' fluid texture, epoxies thicken to a mastic-like consistency. This wood glue is a two-part process, consisting of a resin and a hardener interacting directly during application. Once dried, woodworkers are going to see the toughness and waterproofness of epoxy. Epoxies, in fact, are often go-to wood glues to connect wood into boats.

Clean, dry, and sanded surfaces are the perfect way for Epoxy glue to work. To remove any dust, wax, or other contaminants, wipe off your wood with the correct cleaner. Then, the surfaces need to be gently buffed with towels of paper and air-dry. Finally, make sure your wood is ready to be sanded. Then your two-part epoxy can be mixed and applied as the package instructions say. If you connect two surfaces, you must have a wood clamp handy. Although epoxies are known to be non-toxic, they can cause rash and burns. So, you need to wear gloves and keep your hands out of your eyes and ears.

HOW LONG DOES WOOD GLUE LAST?

Wood glue could last years. Yet you may have learned that PVA wood glue goes bad after a long time it has been frozen or sat around. The reality is that all of this can always happen. Try to mix all the glue particles with a stick (don't just shake). If it is a little dense, add up to 5 per cent vapour. This method is possibly right to use if glue flows easily from the flask and feels slippery between your fingertips – not stringy or sloppy. Yet throw it out if you are in doubt. It may not worth the chance.

Sanding and Preparing Wood Before Staining

A little fundamental knowledge about sanding and about wood preparation before staining, helps to make a staining job quicker and easier.

Sandpaper or Power Tools

The sandpaper grade or grate is dependent on the number of sand granules per square inch of paper. The more numerous, the better the grade. Lower grades mean grosser sandpaper. The numbing is generally written on the back of each sheet.

Medium and fine sandpaper grades are commonly used for furniture and antiques finishing. Coarse greys (those below # 100) harm the wood's fine finish. Medium grains, including # 120 and # 150, are useful to remove old or scratching finishes. Fine grains, like # 220, are also used for final light sanding just before the stain is added to the wood.

Power instruments make sanding easier, but heavy-duty instruments such as belt sanders are built for heavier carpentry and can easily ruin fine antiques. A palm sander is best suited for refinishing.

For fine finishes and delicate pieces, hand-sanding is preferable. Tear the fourth sheets of sandpaper and then fold them into parts just large enough to hold them with three fingers. By wrapping a piece of sandpaper around a block of wood that fits in your hand, you can build a make-up sanding aid. Still better, if you can use a contoured sand block that can be placed in hardware stores by putting the ends into a groove on each end of the block.

Sand with the Grain

Closer examination of a wood piece shows pores in the surface, creating a grain pattern. Sand often perpendicular to or at an angle in the direction of the grain. It also happens when working on corners and corners that are difficult to hit. Scratches made by sanding the grain will look unattractive on the finished portion and will be obvious after staining.

Place the piece in such a way that the surface is horizontal and comfortable. Keep the sanding block flat for a smooth finish, apply even pressure firmly when you are going in the same direction as the grain. Excessive pressure or the corners of the sanding block produce excessive wood depressions.

If using a Palm Sander, the same rules must be applied: sand with the grain and keep the sander flat against the wood, if needed, press.

REMOVING THE DUST

Wood dust from sanding can cause problems if it is not removed before staining the surface. The most effective dust removal devices are not dry rags or brushes. Use a tack cover, a specially made sticky cheesecloth, instead. Remove dust from the folded tackle cloth over the wood. When every side is covered with dust, replenish the tissue to reveal a new surface. In hardware stores, costly tack cloths are present, or you can make your own by soaking a 12 "cheesecloth in a small amount of petroleum oil. Store tack cloths in a plastic bag that are sealed to keep them from shrinking between uses.

Most of the wood dust produced by the sanding is transported, so wearing a particle mask is wise during work.

List of Woodworking Projects for Beginners

Woodwork doesn't have to be scary! Many of these fun, creative projects use scrap lumber and require only basic instruments and a few simple instructions. Tackle one of these starting carpentry plans, and we promise that you will take itchy steps.

WOODEN CUTTING BOARD

To make your own cutting board, you will need untreated hardwood (we used oak), a circular saw, or table saw, sandpaper, food-grade mineral oil and a clean cloth. Be sure that the hardwood you choose is untreated if you plan to use your cutting board for cooking. If you are unsure, just ask someone at your local lumber yard. And for the mineral oil, make sure you use food-grade (most are food grade). It's sometimes called cutting board oil or butcher block oil.

Step One. Draw your board template. When you only use a circular saw, you have to stick to straight-edged designs. Sometimes we love to make a heart-shaped cutting board, but first, we must invest in a table saw. We tried to use a jigsaw, but the oak was too large and difficult to handle safely for our little jig. Yet some use a jigsaw with other (slightly softer) woods or maybe a stronger, more expensive saw.

Step Two. Cut the template out. Make sure your saw manual is read, and all safety information is followed. When the pattern has been cut, sand the edges with medium-grain sandpaper.

Step three. Clean the cutting board so that there's not dust. Use a clean tissue to use the mineral oil. Wipe in the direction of the grain of the wood. For more advice and dry time ideas, search in the bottle. Our mineral oil indicated that before it was ready for cooking, so we coat the cutting board with 3-4 coats with oil.

Step four. How to take care of the cuts: Never immerse a cutting table in soapy water or put through a washing machine. It is safe to wash wooden cutting boards often by hand (and with other wooden cooking utensils). Give your cutting board every 3-6 months a fresh coat of mineral oil to retain a fresh and new look.

DIY PET BED

SUPPLIES

3 – 1x4x8 furring strips

2 – 1x2x8 furring strips

1 – 2x4x10 furring strips

STEP 1 – BUILD THE BASE

Start with cutting. The base of this bed is made of 5 2 pcs, each 22" in length. I've used my Kreg Jig to add them to each. I used 1 1/2" stickers and 2 1/2" stickers.

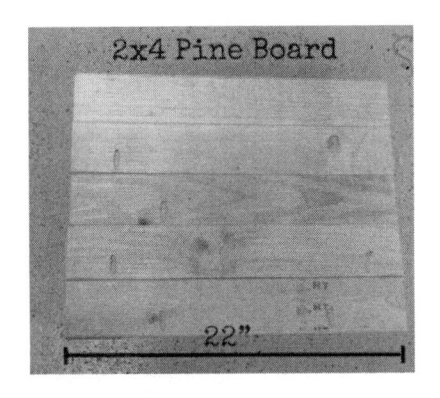

STEP 2 – BUILD THE BACK

The back of the bed is made of 1 to 4 sheets. I made three cuts, each 22" wide. For connect the frames, I used 3/4" pocket holes and 1 1/ 4" pocket hole screws. You can see my pocket holes below.

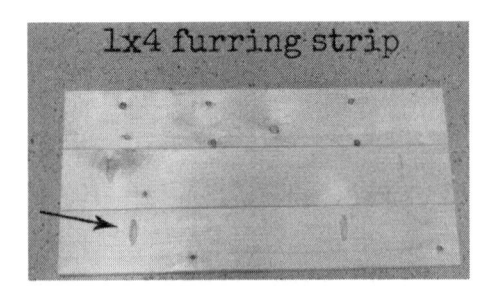

STEP 3 – ATTACH THE BACK

I used my Ryobi AirStrike Nailer to connect the back to the foundation. On the back like this, I ran a Gorilla Wood Glue thread.

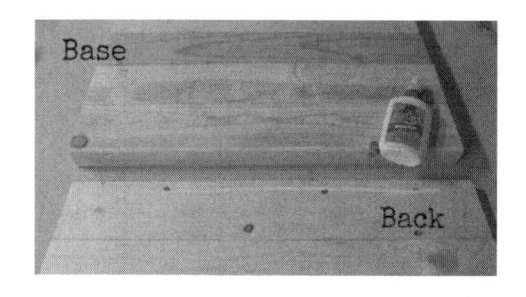

Then, I used 1 1/2" nails to attach it like this.

STEP 4 – BUILD THE SIDES

To make our sides now: can side use three one to 4" paddle strips cut to 18.25" and two 1 to 2" paddle stripes cut to 10.25" respectively?

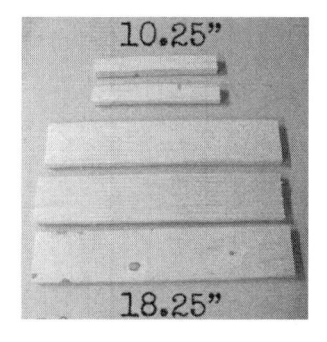

As below, I lined my boards and ran a wood glue line down each leg.

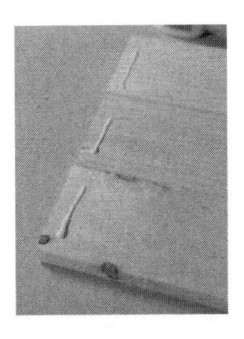

Last, on either end, I used my cordless nailer to repair 1 à 2.

All sides are therefore going to need two 1 to 2" reductions at 15.25". When making these reductions, I like to weigh. Wood is still tiny, and I find that if I calculate as I go, I get the most accurate cuts instead of a cut list. To add the bits to the top and to the bottom, I used wood glue and my nailer.

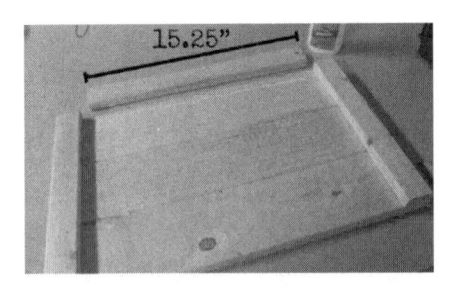

STEP 5 – ATTACH THE SIDES

After I built both sides, I connected them back and forth to the frame. I put the foundation on this side and ran a wood glue line to the top.

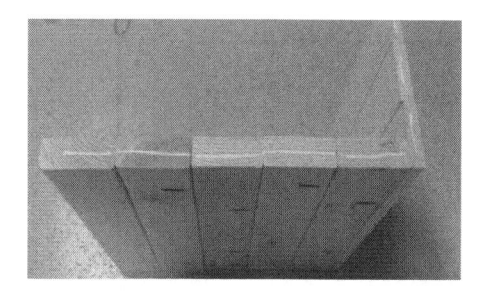

First, I've used my 2" nails nailer for connecting the ends. Do not scrimp on the glue of your wood. Basically, the nails keep everything in place until the glue dries.

That's what my end looks like.

repeat the same thing with the other side piece

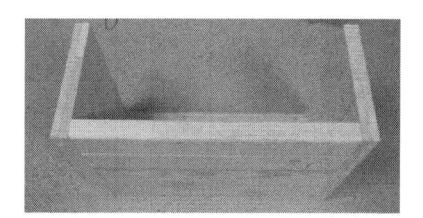

STEP 6 – BUILD THE FRONT

I used a 1 bis4 cut at 24" for the front wall, where his name was going to be. I used wood glue and my nailer all over to patch it.

STEP 7 – BUILD THE FEET

Time for feet! The feet are also made with 1×4. I cut four pieces at 4" long each

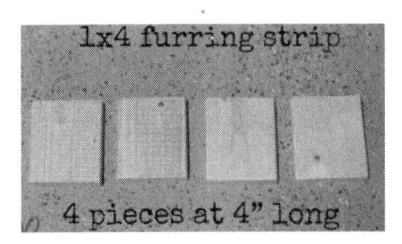

I used wood glue and my nailer with 1 1/4" nails to attach each one at the corners.

STEP 8 – APPLY A FINISH

It needs only one coat and dries in less than an hour, as does Rust-Oleum.

I used my Ryobi Corner Cat sander for distressing the edges until dried out.

With the mark on the crayon, I glued a circle on the front of the 1 to 4 with the tape of a painter.

DIY WOOD DOORMAT

What you need:

– two – 1×4 cedar boards

– table saw

– miter box

– nail gun (or hammer & nails)

– wood glue

– sandpaper

How to make it:

Split 1 to 4 by half with the table saw. Cut a slice of your frame cedar board thickness (we were at 13/16). Measure and decide the duration of your container. We made our own of 18"x29". Cut 45-degree angles on either end of the frame pieces by using the miter box. Clue the frame and weld it together. Cut the board at an angle of 45 degrees, place the corner part firmly on your side, and mark the other end you have to cut. Break the piece inside the frame in another 45-degree angle, glue and nail it. Repeat until the frame is complete. (We used two small pieces of wood just to maintain the distance between the boards). Clean the sides and the boards between them.

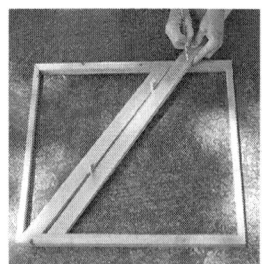

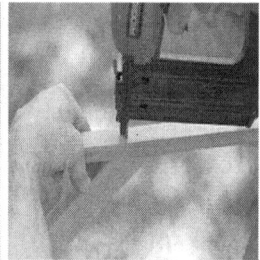

WOODEN BEER CADDY

Essential skills: Advanced novice, you will have some experience with the appropriate resources. Some of it cut straight lines, but you're going to have to shape by hand. It's not hard, but just be careful if you're an absolute newbie.

This DIY wooden beer caddy is a perfect treat for your party enthusiasts. In reality, we made many presents, but we also arranged a party for ourselves. We can bring in it any bottled drink – not just water!

What's the beer carrier you care about? This can be achieved in six basic steps:

- Make Your Cuts
- Shape the Handle
- Cut Angles
- Nail Pieces Together
- Sand
- Finishing

Wood to Use

For this wooden beer caddy, we suggest poplar. Working with poplar is so simple, and it is light and water-resistant (for sucking bottles). It also stains very well.

When you want to make your project a little easier, just use pine. You can use any kind of wood – poplar is one of our favourites.

Were you ready to see the tutorial for the project?

Gather These Supplies

- 1/2" x 6" x 4' poplar hobby board
- 1/4" x 3" x 4' poplar hobby board
- 1/4" x 1 1/2" x 4' poplar hobby board
- 3/4" brad nails
- Wood glue
- Sandpaper
- Danish oil or stain
- Tack cloth
- Wall-mounted bottle opener (with two screws)

Tools

- Miter saw or circular saw
- Power drill
- Jigsaw
- 18-gauge nailer
- 1" Forstner bit
- Phillips bit

Step One: Cut the boards using your saw according to the following measurements

1/4" x 1 1/2" board – cut into five pieces: (1) 7 3/4", (4) 8 3/4" in length

1/4 x 3" board – cut to 7 3/4" length

1/2" x 6" board – cut into three pieces: (1) 7 3/4" in length, (2) 9" in length

Step Two: Form the handle. You 're going to mark 7 3/4" x 3" wooden piece (with a crayon) from the top 1/4" and then 2 1/2" on each side. Then use your Forstner bit for two-hole drilling. Attach them to lines at the top and bottom of the circles, then cut the lines to construct a handle with a puzzle.

Step Three: Cut the angles. Label each side 5 1/2" from the bottom on your 9" pieces of wood. Label the centre and use a 1 1/2" strip on either side of the middle of each piece. Attach both points to a straight edge and use a puzzle to cut the angles

Step Four: Nail pieces together. Use your brad nailer to nail the frame fully together. Put wood glue on the angled sides of the foundation and secure with the nailer.

Align the piece with 7 3/4" on top of the handle. Stick together. Place the handle in position on the sides with wood glue and screw. Attach wood glue and nail in the spot on 8 3/4" sides.

Step Five: Sand the whole caddy with 80 grey sandpaper – then switch to 150 and 220 grey sandpaper to make them smooth.

Step Six: Terminate your wooden beer caddy with staining or oiling and then add your bottle opener with the screws. We had only silver

screws, so we brushed them a little bit with brownish-black paint.

Tip: Use the watered-down acrylic paint in a dark colour just to stain if you do not / want to buy stain for your beer carrier. This fits well and is much cheaper than buying a whole stain, but only if you can make one.

VINTAGE STEP STOOL

Dimensions

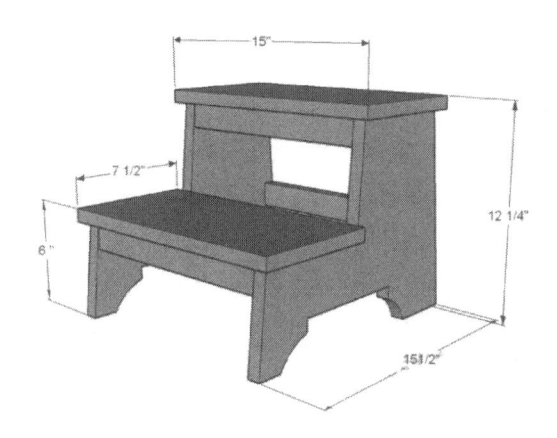

Preparation

SHOPPING LIST

1 – 1×12 @ 32″ (Sides)

1 – 1×2 @ 50″

1 – 1×8 @ 32″ (Treads)

2″ screws or 1 1/4″ pocket hole screws

wood glue, wood filler and finishing supplies

CUT LIST

2 – 1×12 @ 15 1/2" (Sides – cut out in step 1)

4 – 1×2 @ 12 1/2" (Supports)

2 – 1×8 @ 15" (Treads)

STEP 1

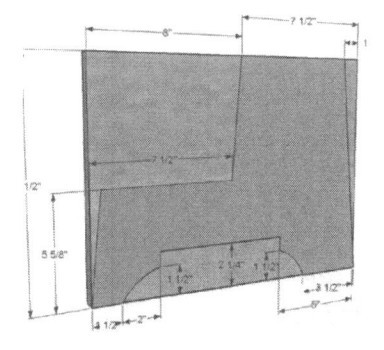

Sides

Use the above ratios to cut the 1x12s as above. Use a puzzle. When you have cut it off, on the other hand, using it as a guide, take note of which side of the line and take your time off. Rims of sand so that the two bits are the same.

STEP 2

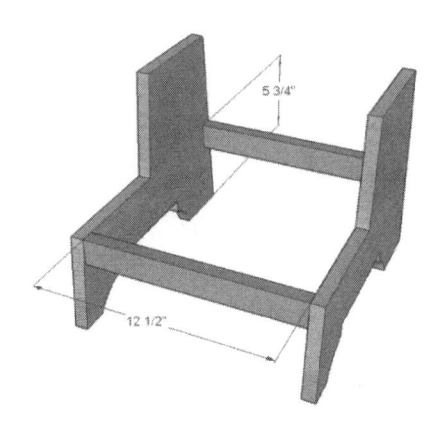

Bottom Supports

Stick with screws and glue the bottom supports. I used pocket hole screws, but 2" wood screws and a good old countersink bit are also suitable for this step.

STEP 3

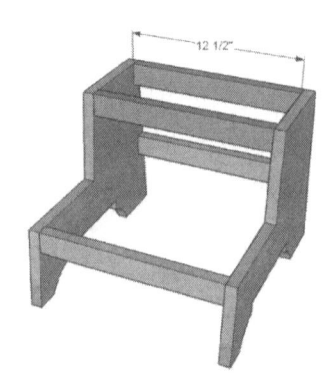

Top Supports

Connect the top supports as the bottom supports.

STEP 4

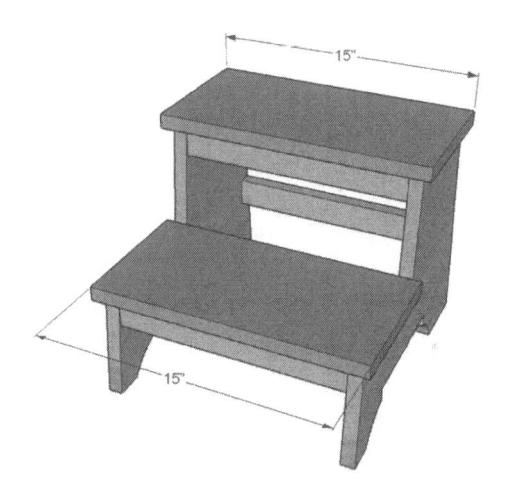

STEP 5

Finishing

Now there is the fun part. I love to paint and complete smaller pieces. I invite you to try your step stool for an impossible end. You should also apply a new paint coat!

WOODEN SOFA SLEEVE WITH CUP HOLDER

Tools:

-clamps (at least 8" long)

- Hole saw in your choice of diameter (based on the most popular cup diameter) A larger hole saw requires the use of a drill press. I used a 3 7/8" hole to see if I had this arbour attached. My hole saw was too wide to be handle with a power drill, so I used the drill press of a friend to cut the hole. For more detail, see phase two.

-tape measure

-pencil

-power drill

Optional tool:

–Kreg pocket hole kit – This is an optional device shown in steps 4 and 7 that adds strength and life to your couch, but is likely unnecessary for a sofa slat that is easy to use.

Materials:

–grade 0000 steel wool

-polyurethane

-wooden board cut into three equal lengths

-piece of thin plywood

-wood glue

-wood stain

–150 grit sandpaper or 180 grit sandpaper

Optional Materials:

-veneer tape— When you don't work high-quality hardwood like maple, oak, or poplar, this is an easy way to finish your lumber edges ugly cut. A softer wood like pine is soaking on the cut tops, making them darker. Once you stain, you can opt to iron on the fan band to prevent this.

-1.25" Kreg screws- these optional screws are only required if you intend to add additional support for the pinhole screws in steps 4 and 7. Wood glue would be necessary otherwise.

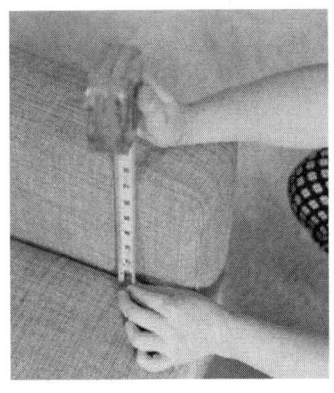

Both the width of the arm and the height. If you don't have the equipment to cut the wood at home, use the following formulas to describe the parts you would need to cut for you at the wood yard. The following calculations suggest that the thickness of the boards used for 1x boards, including 1 t/6 or 1 t/8 board, is 3/4".

Top box — length: 14"/width: arm width + 1.5"

Longitude: 14" / distance: arm height from the coil — you can round down to the nearest board distance.

1/8" piece of plywood — length: arm width/width: arm width (the piece which falls under the cup hole)

My Ikea Karlstad sofa measurements: I used three 14" 1 to 28 lengths of the board and simply trimmed the width to 6.25", the distance I wanted to fit the top piece in my sofa sleeve.

Step Two: Place the hole saw your top piece of wood on one end. Label the middle point where your hole saw pilot drill would start the hole. It's important to remember that you won't be able to handle your drill with your arms as muscularly as you have if you use a big hole saw, as I have done. This will hop around and ruin the wood's finish. I had to carry my piece of wood into the house of a friend to clamp it up and cut the hole with the hammer.

If you don't have a drill press but want to make a hole larger than 2.5", simply miss your hole saw and cut the circle with a puzzle instead.

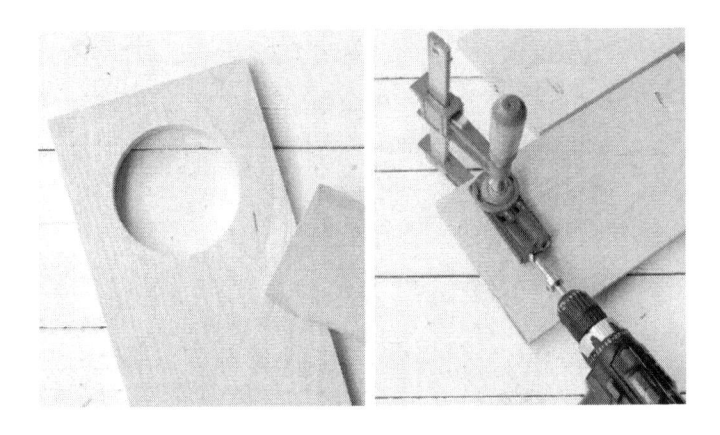

Step Three: Sand inside the opening, the top and bottom of the wood and hold away from corners and edges. When you sand the edges around the corners of the board, the boards will not be smooth when attached in step 5.

Phase 4: This is an optional move. As shown above, clamp up your Kreg jig to drill pocket holes in one end of each side of the board. Just within the sofa sleeve are these pocket holes visible. Once you tie each board together, use the pocket screws offers a secure connection, but is probably not appropriate for the final use of the sleeve.

It is always a good idea to put a pocket hole on scrap wood before you finish it.

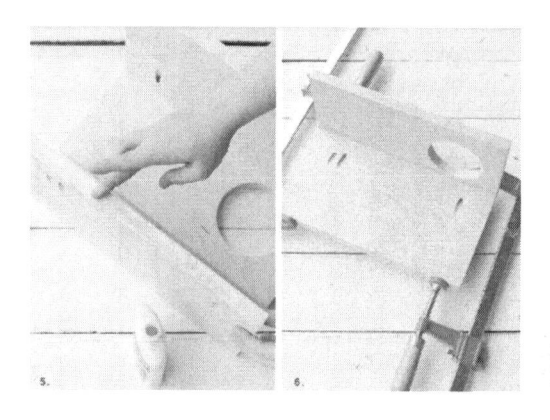

Step 5: Attach a thin wooden sheet of glue to a long edge (the side nearest to your pocket openings if you have decided to use it). Smoothing it with your fingers will help, just clean your fingers in a damp basin.

You will clean the dripping wood glue with a damp rag immediately. Wood glue is very hard to remove, even with strong sanding, after it is dry.

Step Six: Clamp the glued sideboard to the bottom of the top board (set the inside of the board to make pockets). Once you absolutely tighten the clamps, make sure the panels are well balanced at the ends and flush at the corners.

Step Seven: It is an optional move. If you've opted to use pocket screws, it's time to screw them. If the wood parts fall away from one another, wait until the wood glue is completely applied (follow directions on the glue bottle).

Step Eight: Giving the hole part very good sanding after both side parts have been stuck and tightened. There I used 150-grain sandboxes, but you may want to finish off with something closer to the 200 grains if the wood is very soft (like pine) to prevent scratch marks that are highlighted when the stain is added.

Step 9: Allow the piece of wood stain to dry for at least 12 hours until the roughness is gently buffed off with a piece of steel grade 0000. It cuts out the little hair that pops into the wood from the moisture of the paint. If you find that the stain has lightened in certain areas after buffing, you may need to add a bright second colour stain.

Step 10: Use wood glue to connect the square portion of the thin plate to the bottom of the

opening. Make sure that you just add a small amount of glue because the glue gets oozed when you lock it in place. After the plywood has been clamped in, you must quickly clean away the excess glue, or the dried glue becomes evident on the finished product.

Step 11: Cover the sleeve with two light polyurethane coats. This protects it against cup condensation moisture.

MORE PROJECTS TO TRY OUT

- vintage crates
- picture frames
- expansive wheeled coffee table
- DIY Horseshoe Pit
- Rolling Grill Side Cart with Storage
- Scoreboard for Summer Games
- Lounge Chair Build Plans
- DIY Fold-Away Desk from 2x4s
- DIY Inlay Garden Markers
- Easy DIY Tapered Planter
- Simple Modern Coffee Table
- DIY Drawer Dividers for Perfectly Organized Drawers
- How to Build a Farmhouse Sink Base Cabinet
- DIY Tall Nightstand

- Stuffed Animal Storage Bin with Macrame Net
- Gorgeous DIY Necklace Holder from Wood Scraps
- DIY Closet Organizer
- Carved DIY Wood Light Fixture
- Shoe Organizer Tray
- DIY Outdoor Christmas Trees with Lights
- Wooden Advent Calendar with Paper Houses
- Easy Lap Desk with Storage
- Nightstand Valet Docking Station
- Sliding Letter Board
- Wooden Toy Barn
- Nesting Plant Stands

COMMON WOODWORKING PITFALLS AND HOW TO AVOID THEM

You would find it difficult to find a woodworker who did not have something unforeseen that ruined his project (or at least anything that forced himself to do a lot of work to repair it). Below are some of the most common carpentry mistakes and ways of either repairing them or preventing them.

Most mistakes can be absolutely avoided if you slow down. Haste is the most frequent woodworkers' problem. You are rushed and eager to complete a project. Don't do that. Don't do it. Not only you are much more likely to harm your project, but you can harm something much more important – yourself. The number one cause of workplace accidents is hurrying.

If you feel like hurrying things, take a break and note that hurrying could take you longer in the long run if you need to repair an error or go to the emergency room.

UNEVEN OR BLOTCHY FINISH

Often you get tangled finishes from an oil finish like Danish oil or paint. The finish is blotchy as pores in some trees, including cherry, suck in different quantities of oil and look rough.

You can't rectify this until the damage is done, so you must make sure you prepare it in advance. This question can be avoided in two ways:

Using a sanding sealer or other pores to fill the wood pores before the final filling is applied.

Using a polish on top of the wood instead of absorbing it. Two examples are varnish and shellac.

DRAWERS OR DOORS THAT DON'T FIT

Nothing is more heartbreaking than completing your cabinetwork and preparing to glue the drawer into the cabinet for coming to end and find out that the drawer is too large to match the opening. Don't get stuck there and feel puzzled about why it happened. You followed the plans, after all, right?

The question is that you have been ignoring the plans. Here's the situation: If you create a cabinet carcass, the measurements here and there, for example, can be off by 1/32 inches. When you are attempting to put together the carcass, very minor differences will make your drawer not match.

The answer is simple: wait until the drawers or doors are completely done after your carcass. Then forget the scale of the design and function from the carcass. It means the measurements of your drawer or door match those of the carcass.

A TABLE THAT ROCKS

Most often than not, you will find that when you finish making a table, it wobbles. (It might not be acknowledged, however, that most woodworkers have had the same experience.)

In order to prevent this problem, make sure both legs are cut exactly the same length. Put them in a panel cutting jig and run them all simultaneously through the table saw. You do need to ensure that when you stick it up, you get the table square. Assemble the table leg/rail assembly in two steps: firstly, glue the short rails into the legs and then insert these two assemblies into long rails after having a chance to dry entirely. Look for squares in both directions — around the top of the mount and from the lower leg to the opposite top of the head.

Seek to square all from the beginning, some problems that arise. In order to repair a wobbly table after glue-up, change the leg length until it is even. Place the table on a flat bench to see which leg is the longest. First, push the table to the bench of this long leg. Move the leg closely towards the bench edge and level the surface. If this is the long leg, the tabletop will extend out slightly. Use a knife, mark the point at which the top of the bench crosses the table leg. To shorten the leg to that level, use a sander or a plane.

Stain that doesn't take

The most common reasons for not taking a stain are that you have used a wood filler that doesn't fill or have some glue that you didn't completely wipe off when you installed the piece.

Both problems are easy to prevent, but not easy to repair. So, ensure that you use a wood filler which can take stain and clean off all the glue which sprinkles from a joint when assembled.

When your project leads to a non-tuned spot, use coloured glaze (semi-transparent solution similar to thin paints or stains) in the non-tuned surface, change the colour and the cover until it suits the stained wood. Let it dry, then cover it.

Sanding that makes the wood fuzzy

Many of the trees, like birch, become soft if you sand too much. The wood fibres tear and produce gritty flushes on the wood surface. In that state, you don't want to stain or topcoat wood.

When the wood is soft, go down grain or two with sandpaper (120 grit is a good starting place) and sand the fur out. The way to stop fluffy wood is to make sure that you're not sanding with more than 150 grains of paper. Yet neither use a scraper.

JOINTS THAT DON'T FIT TOGETHER

You have done a lot to get close joints, but it does not work when you put the glue on and try to pull them together. Either you have too close joints, or you have joints that just partially pull together and have a 'lock-up.'

Also, dry first to prevent overly close joints. When you have to pound (or tap) the joints together with a briefcase, you should loosen the joints before applying glue. Shave the tenon down slightly if the joints are a mortise and tenon before you can pull the joints by hand or with minimal tapping.

When you lock the joints, you have to tap seriously and clamp it again before the drive. You can't be able to get it to bud, depending on how long the joints are locked. Only stop a locked joint first, as simple as putting the joint together completely when you try to mount it first. Resist the temptation of connecting the joint partially. Also, add a joint before switching to another joint.

TABLETOPS THAT AREN'T FLAT

Once you have made every effort to pick, fry and mount a tabletop, you remove the clamps – just to find that the tabletop is not smooth. You would have two potential explanations for your question if your timber weren't bent, cupped or twisted. Either the edges of the board were not perfectly straight, or the clamp pressure was too high when the boards were glued together.

Make sure you use a joiner that is designed to render perfectly square edges on the board to prevent such problems. Don't press the clamps so hard that the board starts deflecting from the clamps. A lock or two on top of the boards can also help.

You have to plane and sand it down to smooth an irregular tabletop. You lose thickness on the wall, so maybe you don't want to go this direction. Your only choice is to cut off the top of the joints and restart. Take a deep breath – it isn't as bad as it sounds, and it's much easier than flattening with a plane and a sander.

Once again the boards have been removed, attach them, so they have square edges, stable edge joints and test for flat and then force them to place the boards together with enough strength.

WOOD THAT SPLITS WHEN BEING CUT

Running a wooden piece through a saw can cause the spinning blade to break out, as a result of the unstable edge of the wood as the board leaves the saw. Tear-out takes place on the back of the boards as you cut grass.

The way to avoid tear-out is by positioning the rear edge of the wood when it is sliced. The back-up wall serves as a tear-out sacrifice frame. Even, if you have both a rip and a cross-cutting surface, make the first and second rip cross-cutting. Since it is doubtful that the blade would break on a rip cut, you don't need to think about a back-up wall.

Joints that are too loose

A joint often suits too loosely. The loss of flexibility is a particular difficult issue if you deal with mortise and tenon joints because their strength depends on their tightness between mortise and tenon.

So what do you do if the tenon in the mortise is too loose? Okay, apart from cutting a new tenon, it works a lot an adhesive that fills the gaps. Standard wood glue carpenters won't work. You need an epoxy resin adhesive, a two-part adhesive that is sometimes growing to fill the wood gaps.

The other choice is to glue a thin piece of wood into the tenon and then cut it to match the mortise.

CONCLUSION

Once you are done, it's very important to clean up the mess! There are other things you can do to minimize the mess you make when working, such as keeping the sawdust indoors to a minimum.

Ensure that you clean up and wash all your devices. If you use glue or varnish, you may want to ensure that these things do not dry between projects.

If you have any leftover scrap wood from something you have made and built, you will want to set up some storage and organization to use these materials for a future project.

Now that we have covered all the elements of the woodwork for beginners, you are ready to dive in and start building!

And of course, once you have learned the fundamentals of woodworking, you will be able to explore the more advanced woodworking techniques that you can learn to develop and improve your skills.

Within this guide, I tried to cover the most critical aspects of woodwork for beginners. Seek to be consistent with all the above details, and I am very certain that you will enjoy this exciting journey.

Do Not Go Yet; One Last Thing To Do

If you enjoyed this book or found it useful, I'd be very grateful if you'd post a short review on Amazon. Your support does make a difference, and I read all the reviews personally so I can get your feedback and make this book even better.

Thanks again for your support!

Printed in Great Britain
by Amazon